LAW
SPORT ACTIVITY
AND
RISK MANAGEMENT

ROBERT W. KOEHLER
Illinois State University

Copyright © 1987, 1988
STIPES PUBLISHING COMPANY

Published By
STIPES PUBLISHING COMPANY
10 - 12 Chester Street
Champaign, Illinois 61820

Dedicated to those who have been a constant source of encouragement — family, friends and students. Thanks.

TABLE OF CONTENTS

INTRODUCTION

This book is prepared with the professional educator, especially the physical educator and coach, in mind. It is not intended to be legal opinion or a status report on what the current law is. It is intended to provide a synopsis of what some lawyers, legal scholars, judges, case reports and legal resources have to say about physical education, sport, athletics and the people who work in those areas.

It is an attempt by an educator to assist other professionals with their understanding of the *legal aspects of physical education and sport*. "A Schoolman in The Law Library," by A.A. Renzy and M.K. Remmlein, reflects the intent of *Law, Sport Activity and Risk Management*.

A functional knowledge of law, physical education and sport should make for a more confident and poised professional. The sport specialist, whether teacher or coach, should feel comfortable searching through legal resources, reading cases and sampling the opinions of legal scholars, while gleaning ideas for improving the professional environment and learning atmosphere in physical education and sport. The concerned professional will be attuned to what should or should not be done legally. The great fund of cognitive information in law can then be used to the advantage of physical education and sport. And the professional will view his or her knowledge in law and sport activity to be essential and a valuable asset.

Hopefully, the information in this book will help shape a positive approach to the legal resolution of social conflict in sport activity. To facilitate this positive approach, there are a few administrative theories which should be kept in mind:

1. Philosophy determines structure and form gives rise to flow. Are processes different between bosses and leaders? Why? Are autocratic administrative units functionally different than democratic units? Why?
2. "Conflict is not necessarily a wasteful outbreak of incompatabilities but a normal process by which socially valuable differences register themselves for the enrichment of all concerned." (Follett)

1

3 ways to deal with conflict:

1. *Domination*—victory for one side; humiliation for the other.
2. *Compromise*—each side gives up something to insure peace.
3. *Integration*—discover significant aspects of the conflict; not the dramatic ones; a place is found for each desire and neither side loses; both sides gain. (Follett).

3. "Decisions are always made within a framework of certain organization purposes which themselves embody the product of previous decisions." (Barnard)
4. "Mechanism of Influence: people in organizations are not passive instruments or neutral means; they are decision making organisms or mechanisms. Each participant will remain in the organization if the satisfaction utility he derives from the net balance of inducements over contributions (measured in terms of their utility to him) is greater than the satisfaction he could obtain if he withdrew." (Simon)
5. "The individual occupies or enacts a role or roles in a work group within the organization, which in turn functions within a culture." (Getzel)

Essentially, we handle our professional obligations and problems with regard to our basic beliefs about matters (philosophy), how we resolve matters (conflict resolution), how we influence people on the job (mechanism of influence), how we provide leadership (decision making), and how we relate to others (interaction). How well we handle these will determine the extent of our need for legal resolution.

2

CHAPTER I
Law, Behavior, Function

Law

Black's Law Dictionary offers the following definition: Law is 1) a system of principles or rules of human conduct. In this sense it includes decisions of court and acts of legislature. 2) An enactment of a legislature, a statute. The definition addresses two types of law, that being ruling case law, precedent or common law; and written law, enactment, or statutes, the aspects of law which are more formal, systematized and recorded. However, it also implies another aspect of law, and that is a behavioral aspect, rules of and for human conduct, not systematized or recorded.

Behavior

The common phenomena or social dimension which develops between individuals as an unwritten understanding of expected behavior is often slighted in our perception of law.

"Dad sure laid down the law to us", or "I am going to lay down the law if you're not in by . . .", or "I'm telling you that's the way its going to be," or "What I say goes," these statements have been common to people in a variety of settings: the family, personal relationships, group action and play. They were usually stated or proclaimed with assertiveness or force to ensure certain patterns of conduct within the family or team. In effect, the proclamation implying a norm of behavior became law, especially if the infraction led to grounding or suspension from the team.

A cock of the head, a frown, a stare, the mischievous child is eyeballed and possibly behavior changed because of the impending consequence if the perceived rule of conduct is not followed.

Hoebel, "The Law of Primitive Man", expresses several concepts which help one to understand law beyond its formal dimensions. He expresses concepts relative to norms, basic elements and functions of law.

When a sufficient number of responses occur to a specific stimuli we refer to it as a normative response, a norm or ways. Hoebel says, "Law consists of specially demarked set of social norms that are maintained through the (action) application of legal sanction. He also maintained that law is not sharply separable from all other forms of human action (Hoebel). *A social norm is legal if its neglect or infraction is regularly met in threat or fact by the application of physical force by an individual or group possessing the socially recognized privilege for so acting* (Hoebel). When a youth does not keep the hours, the grounding of the youth or suspension of privileges (by threat or fact) by the parent(s) would establish the rule of conduct for that family. Or, a law is established within that unit. A similar scenario could be established for the expected norm of behavior of an athlete as established by the coach through training rules. Law could also be a result, conduct could be regulated.

However, a second aspect must also exist if law is to result. The additional phenomena is enforcement. Law is a principle or rule of conduct so established as to justify a prediction with reasonable certainty that it will be enforced by courts if authority is challenged (Hoebel). The significant factor here for law in the informal sense is the *prediction of enforcement*. If the athlete can predict with reasonable certainty that the coach (authority) will exercise some enforcement if the training rule is broken, then the training rule will become a principle or rule of conduct (law) for the team.

Accordingly, law (in a formal sense) comprises or satisfies four elements: 1) normative, 2) regularity, 3) enforcement and 4) the courts (Hoebel). And, a parallel exists with informal law. *Law* in the *formal* sense is the phenomena (norm) of behavior resulting from the threat or fact of enforcement by others in the social setting, be it parent, coach, or partner.

Function

Whether it be by legislative enactment or perceived rules of behavior, law becomes a response to social need. Unfortunately, as implied, the law is usually a step behind the need. It's the need to promote, regulate or control desired behavior that has brought about the response, LAW. And without making a value judgement on culture or societies, it should be recognized that all cultures or societies had or have rules of conduct, LAW. Hoebel maintains that "as for law simple societies need little of it (homogeneity gives way to heterogeneity) . . . everything moves to increase potentially for conflict. The more civilized man becomes the greater is man's need for law and the more law be creates." (Hoebel) Basically, simple societies may have fewer laws and complex societies may have more.

4

Although history can well document the ages and stages of man's development from the Agrarian age to the machine age, societies need not have passed the successive stages of development from a simple to a more technical society to have complex laws. A simple society could suddenly find itself engulfed by a more complex system i.e. primitive tribes being assimilated into a modern society because of technological growth and population expansion. The most recent examples where two different law systems, both in number and degree, have come into conflict would be the natives of the Amazon as prospectors seek their fortune, or the Ilongots of the Phillippines, or the Eskimos. One society having few laws and another having complex laws.

It is possible that this same concept of simple law exists in the world of sport. Small teams, or small groups of performers need very few rules and regulations, individual sports as contrasted with team sports. Informal rules of conduct would be established through personal contact, respect and threat of loss or promise of gain as a result of conduct. The larger teams or groups may feel the need for more rules or written codes of performance.

In this context, small teams or groups regulate conduct by informal laws and large groups by more formal laws. Regardless, it should be understood that physical education and sport function with a myriad of rules or laws; rules of the game or sport, rules or principles of training and development, laws of Physics (i.e. motion), eligibility rules, and Laws of Learning to mention only a few. *Physical education, athletics, and sport are indeed rules oriented.* They're inundated with rules (law); the application of which is to insure success in performance; the development of which is a response to social need.

If law is a response to social need, then it has specific functions. And, more often than not, the function is usually generalized as "to protect". However, in Hoebel's view, primitive or simple societies were maintained by four functions of law, four functions which are still applicable in the modern era. These four functions (Hoebel) of law can be summarized as follows:

- to define relationships among members of society, to assert what activities are permitted or what ruled out.
- taming of naked force and directing force to the maintenance of society
- disposition of troubled cases as they arise.
- define relations between individuals and groups as conditions of life change.

Examples in sport and physical education parallel to these functions are not difficult to find. Title IX legislation certainly *defined relations* between individuals and groups establishing equal opportunity for participation in sport for women and by regulating against sexual bias. The same *permitted participation in some activities* and *ruled out* participation in other activities for both women and men. The large crowds at some special sports events, especially international soccer, pose a problem of *taming the naked force* of the onrushing crowd. Crowd control and facility legislation has resulted. Political protest or demonstration is naked force controlled by permits. It's legislated and permitted through the freedom of speech and expression statute. *Troubled cases* relative to violence in sport (hockey, or the Tomjonavich incident in pro-basketball) have been recent in the courts. An extensive list of topics posing troubled cases could be made: dress code, drug usage, amateur status, contracts, handicapped participation, product liability, pass and play litigation and on, and on go the social situations requiring legal response.

Tort

Whereas the types of law were identified as statuatory (enacted) and common (case), we can also identify criminal and civil actions in law. Criminal action is the state against a person(s) for the protection of the people, and a civil action is a person against a person(s) for the recovery of damages. The particular focus of our concern in Sport and Physical Education is civil action . . . one brought to recover some civil right or obtain redress for some wrong (Black), especially tort.

Tort is a group of situations or relationships recognized as civil wrongs for which the courts afford remedy, usually in the form of action for damages; a breach of a duty, other than one arising out of contract, giving rise to a damage action; an unlawful violation of another's legal rights; legal enforcement of moral standards of conduct (Liebee).

The term tort is derived from the Latin tortus which means twisted . . . activity which in some way deviated from normally accepted patterns of behavior. One might ask, twisted from what? Twisted from the norm of behavior expected for the circumstance by a reasonable person.

A norm of sport behavior may be safe performance as compared to reckless behavior:

Nabozny v. Barnhill 334 N.E. 2d 258 "a recognized set of

6

rules governs the conduct of competition; and a safety rule is contained therein which is primarily designed to protect players from serious injury. A player is charged with a legal duty to every other player to refrain from conduct prescribed by a safety rule. A reckless disregard for safety of other players cannot be excused." (Gowen:1982)

Summary

- Law is a norm of expected behavior, whether it is in the informal or formal mode.
- Law is but a response to social need.
- Law is essential to the maintenance of societies. The more complex the society the greater the need for law.
- Principles or rules of human conduct (formal) are not sharply separable from all other forms of human conduct or behavior (informal).
- Law functions to resolve troubled cases, tame naked force, define relationships asserting what activities are permitted or ruled out, and defining relationships as society changes.
- Law is often a step behind society and social change.
- Tort is a group of situations or circumstances recognized as civil wrongs for which the court affords remedy, activity which in some way deviates from normally accepted pattern of behavior.

You're In Their Shoes

1. A son or daughter's first date extends well beyond the established hour of return, clothes and breath suggests questionable behavior, and being grounded is a possibility.
   - First date, what is the expected front door behavior?
   - What are the expectations in a relationship?
   - Is the expected norm of behavior a law?
   - When and how does it become law?

2. An academic performance of four A's and a F has resulted in a player being ineligible for sport competition. However, the "no pass, no play" concept is not being equally applied to other units in the school.
   - Is this a norm of behavior for the athlete in and about school, in practice and on the play field?

3. Your team has reached mid season without a loss and with many of the victories determined by the dependable kicking of

your placement specialist from Bavaria. Hard work and adherence to strict training rules, including no drinking of alcohol, has paid off on the playing field. Reports are received from a concerned citizens about the beer drinking habits of your kicking specialist.
  • Does a conflict in social norms of behavior exist, or will the expected norm of behavior result in social conflict?

4. The sauna in the men's locker room has primarily served the wrestling team to facilitate weight loss. And, it was administratively necessary to set regulations to facilitate continuous availability to the traditionally strong wrestling team and its members by prohibiting use to women and some men.
  • Has social change occurred which necessitates redefining of relationships?
  • Is there a need to define relationships, asserting what activity is permitted and what is ruled out?

Risk Management Suggestions

As a parent, teacher, coach or administrator, examine the extent of duty, reasonableness or standard of care associated with any projected norm of behavior to the previous circumstances.
  • make every effort to distinguish norms of behavior which regularly occur and may necessitate modification by the application of some influencing factor.
  • make every effort to identify social change which necessitates redefining of relationships between people.

Selected References

Black, Henry C., *Black's Law Dictionary*, West Publishing Co., St. Paul, Minnesota, 1933.

Gowen, Thomas, "Sports Program and Injuries: Liability Since Rutter," *Pennsylvannia Law Journal-Reporter*, April 5, 1982, Vol.V No. 15.

Hoebel, Adamson E., *The Law of Primitive Man*, Harvard University Press, 1954.

Leibee, Howard C., *Tort Liability For Injuries To Pupils*, Campus Publishers, Ann Arbor, Michigan, 1965.

CHAPTER II
The Problem

During the 1981 Conference on Law and Amateur Sports (Indianapolis), it was proclaimed that, "Sports and law or law and sports are here to stay." The relationship seemed obvious and accepted by all as a matter of fact. The most obvious justification for the enduring relationship of law and sport is social conflict. If law is a response to social need, then liability in physical education and sport reflects an attempt at resolution of social conflict in those areas and, so long as sport remains a part of society, this relationship will persist.

However, there are other reasons, some not so obvious, for persistent problems to exist in athletics, sport and physical education, necessitating legal action.

First, *physical education and sport are activity oriented.* They utilize movement, force, equipment and projectiles in special environments as participants seek to achieve specific goals and/or satisfaction:

- SPEED to get to an object, to be faster than someone or something, or in patterns of play/performance.
- FORCE to lift something, put or throw something, control or subdue something.
- OBJECTS to protect in a static sense (helmet, face mask) or use in motion (bats, clubs, rackets).
- OBJECTS to propel, or set in motion a person or thing (springboards, trampoline, bows, sling shots).
- ENVIRONMENTS such as space (air & skydiving), water (swimming, scuba), ice and snow (skating, skiing), wood, concrete, metal, etc.

These phenomena produce *a varied pattern of risk and hazard* to the participant or others when coupled with human behavior and judgment. Most hazards become dangerous only when humans interact with them. (Thygerson:50) The result is dangerous activity the reasonableness of which may be in question. And, the potential for injury in activity is amplified by the following data:

Each year, sports in America cause over 17 million injuries that require medical attention. (Peterson:10)

9

Eighty-six (86) percent of all high school players will sustain at least one injury at some point in their career. (Peterson:10)

Professionals working in the previously described situations are *called upon to perform a myriad of duties and roles,* sometimes contradictory in relationship: instructor, trainer, playground supervisor, coach, club sponsor, disciplinarian, intramural supervisor, first aid, and usually are called upon in a school emergency.

The *physical activity sciences are disciplines which are heavily "rules" oriented.* As reported in Chapter IV on Rules, Godek said, "those associated with athletics realize that rules play a vital role in sports. All matters relating to the teaching of skills and the ways in which practice sessions are conducted are to a significant degree determined by the rules of the game" (Godek:16). Rules which are intended to regulate behavior in the process can lead to conflict in need of resolution. Dress codes are a prime example of this occurrence.

According to Gauerke 8,000 civil cases involving schools and school personnel occur each year . . . total of 15 million dollars. (Hurt:200)

The *modification of law,* especially at the state level, has created an awareness that school districts can be used. This has resulted in some encouragement to the public, seeking a "deep pocket" for recovery.

Classroom teachers, especially elementary teachers in some states, may need only a minimal background in physical education to teach the subject matter. *Teaching methods and teacher qualifications* can be a conflicting circumstance in need of resolution. As discussed earlier, the sensibility of popular techniques and qualifications of coaches have been seriously questioned.

The health and condition of the participant are overriding factors in all physical activities. Physical educators and coaches should know the health status of the participant to be in activity.

Palos Verde, California insurance premiums for the school district's $6 million liability coverage jumped from $12,000 to $139,000 in three years. One Palos Verde athlete who broke his arm while playing football sued the school district for $50,000, alleging inter alia, that school physicians should have known that his bones were brittle and thereby have barred him from the squad. (Peterson:10)

The *frequency of accidents in the discipline increases* the potential for some legal recourse. Majority of accidents in school occur in physical education, athletics, and recreation, 40% (Yost:8). There are laws requiring Physical Education. Mallois states, ". . . in all 50 states requiring Physical Education, an investigation disclosed 552,000 accidents during one year and over ½ of all injuries were those involved in physical education. (Mallois: 62) In fact, it has been reported that ⅔ of all school jurisdiction cases occur in physical education and related activities. (Yost: 9)

Finally, a basic reason for the problem of liability in physical education and sport is *a change in social attitude*. The period of social unrest during the 1960's is a prime example. The student's rights movement of the 1960's served as a lever for testing the degree of authority to regulate student appearance. (Vacca:235)

This new awareness led to the challenge of all facets of education. Then, Title IX was enacted (1972), and it reflected a change of social attitude toward sport/activity and the right to participate, which also led to litigation. It is recognized that the U.S. population is activity oriented, 90% participate in 1 of 75 sport activities (Yost:7).

Summary
The basic reasons for liability to be a persistent problem in physical education and sport can be listed as follows:
- Physical Education, Athletics and Sport are activity oriented which results in a varied pattern of risks and hazards.
- Professionals (teachers/coaches) are asked to performance a myriad of roles and duties, often contradictory.
- The disciplines are heavily rules (formal and informal) oriented.
- The law has been modified to allow for recovery of damages from schools and school districts.
- The health status of the participant is a meaningful variable in all activity.
- The potential for and frequency of accidents is very high.
- A change in social attitude toward authority and the right to participate.
- A change in social attitude toward activity.

You're In Their Shoes

1. Ten separate drills centered on quick start, stop and change of direction are planned for basketball practice to help stress fundamentals. Players are complaining about "hot" spots on their feet after four drills but numerous repetitions.

• Does the teacher/coach have a duty to modify activity to reduce or minimize risk of injury?

2. During the course of the job interview, you clearly establish strong qualifications in teaching physical education but only a superficial understanding of track and field. You are offered the teaching position with the provision that you will be the head coach in track and field.
   • Does a professional create risks by assuming duties which they feel qualified to perform but lack the credentials and experience to support their act?

3. The physical education class has been undergoing a battery of physical fitness test. Mary has been absent from school and your class for a week but has returned in time to resume the testing and start off with a six minute run. The challenge of running a maximum distance in set time can be stressful. Mary has a note from the school nurse allowing her to return to class and activity.
   • Is it reasonable for a student to return to full activity on the basis of a note or voucher without an assessment by the physical activity specialist on the readiness of the student to perform?
   • Does the instructor have a duty to be knowledgeable of the health status of the participant prior to involvement in activity?

Risk Management Suggestions

• Identify the risks and hazards associated with the situation:
  nature of the participant
  nature of the activity
  nature of the environment
  nature of the equipment
  nature of the methods and procedures.

• Reduce and/or remove all risks and hazards associated with the situation, where feasible.
• Compensation for all risks and hazards that cannot be removed (example, using pads, fences, cages, restraints, etc.).
• Create no additional risks or hazards through the modifications in preparation for performance or the performance itself.
• Develop methods and techniques to reduce the frequency of accidents.
• Develop recordkeeping techniques on all participants to include

data essential prior to performance, while in the performance mode and post performance information.

- Develop methods and procedures for assessing and monitoring the health status of all participants.

Selected References

Hurt, T.W., "Elements of Tort Liability as Applied to Athletic Injuries," *The Journal of School Health,* April 1976, Vol XLVI, No. 4., pp. 200-202.

Mallois, H.C., "The Physical Educator and the Law," *The Physical Educator,* May 1975, Vol 32, p. 61.

Peterson, T.L., "The Role of the Lawyer on the Playing Field," Barrister, pp. 10-13, 20.

Thygerson, A., *Essentials of Safety,* Prentice Hall, Englewood, NJ, 1986, p. 50.

Vacca, R. and Hudgins, H.C., *Liability of School Officials and Administrators for Civil Right Torts,* Michie Co., 1982. pp. 225-240.

Yost, C.P., *Sport Safety,* National Education Association, AAHPERD—Division of Safety, Washington, D.C., 1973. pp. 7-9.

CHAPTER III
Negligence

Shop teachers, teachers of science who supervise laboratory work, driver education teachers, *physical education teachers* and coaches of sports are in positions which make them more subject to allegations of negligence for pupil injury than teachers of academic subjects. (Prosser:185) This list should be expanded to include personnel within the recreation leisure services sector: little league coaches, swimming pool managers, aerobic instructors, playground supervisors, etc. This is especially true because of the accident rate and jurisdiction cases that result in the areas. For instance, the National Safety Council report for schools with a representative enrollment of 2,547,000 pupils in 1962 revealed that two-thirds of school jurisdiction accidents occur in physical education and related activities. One study, conducted in a large city in 1956, showed that almost three-fourths of elementary accidents occurred in physical education rooms and on playgrounds. (California:21) And, the frequency of accidents and litigation in the physical activity sciences since those reports has not decreased, but has lead to a TORT CRISIS in the 1980's.

The previously mentioned educators, coaches and professionals are more closely related to pupil activity than are other members of the school staff. They are, therefore, more often named as defendants in case alleging negligence which resulted in injuries to pupils. These tort or civil actions in sport and physical education generally focus on liability (legal responsibility), alleging the defendant is responsible on the grounds of intentional interference resulting in an injury (assault and battery), or the fault of the defendant that the injury occurred (strict liability) or the failure to act as a reasonably prudent person the injury occurred (negligence).

"In civil law, which comes from Roman law and in particular from the Lex Aquilia (Digest IX, 2-7-4), responsibility is founded on the fault and the causal relationship between it and the injury suffered." (Silance: 2)

15

Negligent Behavior

It is necessary to establish or understand what kind of conduct constitutes negligence which would make a coach or teacher (sportucator) liable for damages resulting from students' injuries. According to Rosenfield, "Negligence is the failure to act as a reasonably prudent and careful person would act under the circumstances involved." (Rosenfield:3). Negligence is any conduct which falls below the standard established by law for the protection of others against unreasonable risk of harm. (Rosenfield:3)

It may appear that there is no standard of evaluating behavior in the various situations. (Garber:78) However, he is expected to act in a reasonable and prudent manner; and is liable whether he is present or not. (Garrison:70) The item in question is, *what is reasonable?* The courts have personified the reasonableness test in the "reasonable man." (Alexander and Solomon:596) This helps to function as a standard or guideline.

Reasonableness

Basically, what is reasonable for one person and circumstance may not be reasonable for another person and circumstance. One man's reasonableness may be another man's unreasonableness, vice versa. Therefore, in reality, the reasonable person is nonexistent. "The reasonable man is a hypothetical person, a community ideal of human behavior, whose conduct under the same or similar circumstances is regarded as the measure of reasonable behavior, "A fictitious person who never has existed on land or sea." (Alexander and Solomon:596)

The courts have structured a model or template of behavior standards which may be applied to each situation. The reasonable man . . . possesses the same physical qualities, age, and sex of the defendant. (Hurt:200) Intellectual qualities are usually not given allowance by the court. (Hurt:200) Alexander and Solomon, *College and University Law*, list these characteristics of the reasonable man: 1) the physical attributes of the defendant himself; 2) normal intelligence; 3) normal perception and memory with a minimum level of information and experience common to the community, and 4) such superior skill and knowledge as the actor has or holds himself out as having. (Alexander and Solomon:597) The model would change with different factual situations because of the attributes or deficiencies of the defendant himself and because of peculiarities of beliefs, values and customs of the individual community. (Alexander and Solomon:597)

Parameters in physical education and sport which may impact on and necessitate a varied application of the model are not hard to find. The person in special Olympics or Adapted programs because of a handicap or crippling condition would not be held to the same standard as the person without an infirmity. Likewise, the numerous communities which provide the functional base for teachers and coaches vary in their social personality. The small, rural, conservative community which still reserves one night a week as church night has peculiarities in beliefs different from the larger, more open, affluent community. The standard of expectation would be decidedly different. The coach or teacher would also be expected to have "normal" intelligence, perception and memory. That is to imply typical intelligence, conforming to a norm type, or standard. A comparable term may be "ordinary," characterized as not being uncommon or exceptional, but routine or normal. A review of the standard of care that the person does or does not exhibit as expressed in the degrees of negligence can provide more perspective on reasonableness, normal or ordinary;

> *1st Degree or Slight* Negligence — an absence of the degree of care and vigilance which persons of extraordinary prudence and foresight are accustomed to use; (38 *Am. Jur.*:45-47)
>
> *2nd Degree or Ordinary* Negligence — the failure to exercise such care as the great mass of mankind ordinarily exercises under the same or similar circumstances, (38 *Am. Jur.*:45-47)
>
> *3rd Degree or Gross* Negligence — the injury actually was foreseen, intended and implies utter disregard of consequences as to suggest something of an intent to cause injury. (38 *Am. Jur.*:45-47)

Therefore, the teacher/coach would be expected to reflect the ordinary intelligence, ordinary-perception and ordinary memory.

Significant in the model of reasonable man is the comment about "such superior skill and knowledge as the actor has or holds himself out as having." The activity specialist, teacher or coach, should not hold himself out as having more skill and knowledge than qualifications, credentials and experience reflect. A teacher with limited skills in gymnastics should not include advanced skills and apparatus work without proper qualifications, etc. Additionally, a person may hold himself up as having more skills in a wide variety of ways and should exercise common sense before putting him or herself jeopardy. The Ridge v. San Diego Chargers (filed 1970) is a good example of where qualifications came into question. The case was the first to be heavily litigated on the use of drugs in sports. The trainer, a registered physical therapist was characterized as follows: "Various depositions indicated that *(trainer)* administered injections (an illegal practice for a registered therapist, which (trainer) is); that he kept personal medical records about which Dr. Woodward knew nothing and that he sometimes exceeded Dr. Woodward's orders by giving additional therapy and treatment."

"He is a registered physical therapist, although he should also probably be a registered nurse and a general practitioner, if not an orthopedic surgeon, the medical observer noted." (Washington Post: D 6 Col. 1)

A guideline for the sport activity specialist is, not to make yourself out to be something that you are not.

Behavior

Harper has outlined the types of negligent behavior in such a way as to give general boundaries to the kinds of conduct which creates actionable negligence. An act may be negligent because: (Harper:171)

1. It is not properly done; appropriate care is not employed by the actor.
2. The circumstance under which it is done create risks, although it is done with care and precautions.
3. The actor is indulging in acts which involve an unreasonable risk of direct and immediate harm to others.
4. The actor sets in motion a force, the continuous operation of which may be unreasonably hazardous to others.
5. He created a situation which is unreasonably dangerous to others because of the likelihood of the action of third persons or of inanimate forces.
6. He entrusts dangerous devices or instrumentalities to persons who are incompetent to use or care for such instruments properly.
7. He neglects a duty of control over third persons who, by reason of some incapacity or abnormality, he knows to be likely to inflict intended harm upon others.
8. He fails to employ due care to give adequate warning.
9. He fails to exercise the proper care in looking out for persons whom he has reason to believe may be in the danger zone.
10. He fails to employ appropriate skill to perform acts undertaken.

11. He fails to make adequate preparation to avoid harm to others before entering upon certain conduct where such preparation is reasonably necessary.

12. He fails to inspect and repair instrumentalities or mechanical devices used by others.

13. His conduct prevents a third person from assisting persons imperiled through no fault of his own.

14. His written or spoken word created negligent misrepresentation.

There are really only two areas of inquiry in cases brought on negligent theory, "negligence and contributory negligence and both are resolved by the stand of the reasonably prudent mass." (Gowen:2) Frequently the question arises about the effort exercised by the injured party to provide for his own welfare. Basically, this is CONTRIBUTORY NEGLIGENCE. And, it is defined as failure of the injured party to exercise due care for his own good or welfare. The courts normally hold that one who is contributorily negligent cannot recover damages. (Delon:70) However, in recent years this aspect of law is undergoing change. The legal doctrine of COMPARATIVE NEGLIGENCE has been viewed by some as the fairer and more reasonable approach. "The Illinois Supreme Court . . . has abolished one doctrine of negligence and adapted another. The decision . . . means that a person involved in negligence litigation may collect compensation based on a percentage of his negligence. This is called comparative negligence. Under the contributory negligence law, in effect for nearly a century, a person found to have contributed to an accident can't collect anything. The court abolished this law." (Holliday:D) The *National Education Association Journal*, as early as 1958, reported that Arkansas, Georgia, Mississippi and Nebraska were states which adapted the pro-rating doctrine. (Ware:603) George Peters, a California attorney, predicted in 1980 that many state legislatures would follow the example of California and pass legislation permitting the use of comparative negligence. (Appenzeller:16) The concept that fault for a given circumstances can be *prorated* is comparative negligence and gaining in popularity. The Iowa Court in Goetzman v. Wichern (327 N.W. 2d 742 (Iowa 1982) case stated it this way: "Whatever may have been the historical justification for (contributory negligence), today it is almost universally regarded as unjust and inequitable to vest an entire accidental loss on one of the parties whose negligent conduct combined with the negligence of the other party to produce the loss," Only the pure form of comparative negligence proportions a reduction of recovery to a person's fault in all cases and prevents a party at fault from escaping liability in any case. (National: 50) It has been described by some as being the most logical, most reasonable, fairest and simplest to administer. Regardless, prorating not only determines the percentage of recovery, but in some instances if recovery will or will not be allowed.

Duty

In order to establish negligence PROXIMATE (legal) CAUSE must be shown. This is to say that the teacher and/or coach, had a duty or obligation to the plaintiff. An Illinois case defines proximate cause as:

> What is the proximate cause of an injury is ordinarily a question of fact, to be determined from consideration of all the evidence and attending circumstances; it can arise as a question of law only when the facts are not only undisputed, but are also such that there can be no differences in the judgement of reasonable men as to the inferences to be drawn from the facts; if it could have been foreseen by the exercise of ordinary care that some injury might or would result from an act is a proximate cause of injury. (Danhoff v. Osborne:15)

Prosser explained duty in the following manner: "a duty or obligation, recognized by the law, requiring the actor to conform to a certain standard of conduct, for the protection of others against unreasonable risk." (Prosser:143)

Three primary sources of duty were identified by B. Van Der Smissen, *Legal Liability of Cities and Schools for Injuries in Recreation and Parks.* The sources of duty are 1) inherent in the situation, 2) voluntarily assumed and 3) required by statute. These sources cover duties arising from acting as a professional person, by voluntarily assuming and interpersonal relationship and by legislative enactments, statutes.

Courts have reinforced the concept that teachers owe duty to protect them (students) from injury and harm. Duty may even be greater distinction in one situation as opposed to another. (Mallois:61). Students at the senior high level may expect a particular standard of care from the teacher; whereas, the same activity by elementary students require much greater surveillance. (Mallois:61) The injured party must show that the defendant owned a duty to protect complainant from injury, defendant failed to exercise that duty, . . . this failure was the direct (proximate cause) of the injury, and that actual loss or damage resulted. (DeLon:70) This is to say that 1) a duty existed, 2) there was a breach of that duty, and 3) there was a causal connection between the breach of duty and the injury which occurred. Therefore a valid case in an action for negligence has certain prerequisite conditions or elements: duty, standard of care, proximate cause, and injury. Some general comments in summary of duty and its elements are:

> Duty: an obligation to another may result from 1) *familiarity*, the teacher knew, had this person in school, and was aware of the circumstance or possibility. 2) *Contract*, the teacher or coach obligated by employment to perform in a particular manner. 3) *Assumption*, the individual voluntarily assumed to perform in a particular manner or capacity. 4) Duty may *intensify* as risk increases. As an activity is modified and becomes more hazardous, duty is increased. No general duty to aid may exist even though a moral obligation may be felt. *Foreseeability* of danger imposes an added standard of care. The assumption of duty 5) requires subsequent action to *be reasonable*. 6) Duty may be imposed by the court(s).
> Standard of Care: 1) As foreseeable risk involved increases the standard of care increases. 2) There is a lack of uniformity in care with children and the aged given substantially more leeway. 3) As age, intelligence and experience increase, there is a commensurate increase in the standard of care expected. (Alexander:15-18)
> Proximate Cause: 1) A duty must have existed, 2) the person should, would need to be in the zone of obvious danger, 3) actors force must have been continuous and active up to the actual harm. (Alexander:19)
> Injury: The individual actually suffered an injury or loss or damages as a result of the act. (Alexander:21)

Opinion

A contributing factor to the question of negligence is the fact that the layman considers himself to be an expert attuned to the nature of teaching and coaching. Few profess little ignorance of education, especially physical education and coaching. The general public 'second guesses' coaches and teachers alike with non-professional advice and interference in the academic process and learning atmosphere. Although the 'second guessing' may be done with the best of intent, it is done without hesitation and abounds to a level beyond acceptance in other professions.

"Those that can, do; those that can't, teach," this attitude of the public is root to some of the negligence problems and social conflict in the physical activity sciences.

Summary

- Civil law is founded on the fault and the causal relationship between it and the injury suffered.
- Negligence is the failure to act as a reasonably prudent person would act under the circumstances involved.
- Negligence can be by commission or omission. The person committed an act or omitted (failed to act) an act.
- Negligence is any conduct which falls below the standard established by law for the protection of others against unreasonable harm.
- "Reasonable man" is a fictitious person personified in law by the "test" or model of the reasonable man.
  1. Physical attributes of the defendant himself.
  2. Normal intelligence.
  3. Normal perception and memory with a minimum level of information and experience common to the community.
  4. Such superior skill and knowledge as the actor has or holds himself out as having.

- *Slight negligence* is an absence of the degree of care and vigilance which persons of extraordinary prudence and foresight are accustomed to use.
- *Ordinary negligence* is a failure to exercise such care as the great mass of mankind ordinarily exercises under the same or similar circumstances.
- *Gross negligence*, the injury actually was foreseen, intended and implies utter disregard for consequences as to suggest something of an intent to cause injury.
- The teacher or sport activity specialist should not hold himself or herself up to be something that they are not.
- Harper has identified fourteen types of behavior which may be negligent.
- The failure of an injured party to exercise due care for his or her own welfare is *contributory negligence*.
- *Comparative negligence* proportions a reduction of recovery to a person's fault, or fault for a given circumstance can be prorated.

- Comparative negligence as a trend has been described as the most logical, most reasonable, fairest and simplest to administer.
- Duty is an obligation recognized by law, requiring a person(s) to conform to a certain standard of conduct, for the protection of others against unreasonable risk.
- The elements of PROXIMATE CAUSE are: duty existed, there was a breach of that duty, and there was a causal connection between the breach of duty and the injury which occurred.
- Duty may intensify as risk increases.
- The voluntary assumption of duty requires that the subsequent action be reasonable.
- The general public professes little ignorance of education, especially physical education and sport.

You're In Their Shoes

1. A spectator was traveling along a walkway at a baseball game, when he was injured by a bat that flew out of the batter's hands. The point of injury was eighty feet from home plate and almost to first base.
   - Is it reasonable to furnish protection to the spectator from flying bats, at least in the area where the greatest danger exists?
   - Does the facility manager have a duty to screen dangerous areas, especially where the risk of injury is foreseeable?

2. A high school wrestling official allegedly permitted a participant to continue an illegal hold on his opponent, the opponent becoming paralyzed as a result.
   - Is it reasonable to assume the referee will adequately supervise and control the match?
   - Is it negligent behavior for an official to fail to stop an athletic contest, once begun, due to the physical condition of the playing facility?

3. A high school senior was seriously injured when he ran through a glass panel at the end of the gymnasium. The youth was engaged in basketball wind sprints at the time of injury and knew of the glass panels, because of his previous experience on the team.
   - Even though the wind sprints were being conducted by a coach, did the student have a duty to disregard compliance for his own welfare?

- Does the student have a duty to exercise ordinary and reasonable care for his own safety under known circumstances?
- would the failure to exercise reasonable and ordinary care for his own safety be contributory negligence?

Risk Management Suggestions

- utilize attitude sampling techniques to assess the human relations environment in your classroom, or on your team, or in your school. The instrument could be two phase. Phase I would be a self assessment; whereas, phase II would be the participant assessment. Items of critical concern could be singled out and focused on for thirty days for remediation: i.e.

	Always	Some-times	Seldom
1. Regardless of my personal feelings, I exhibit good will to all my contacts.	_____	_____	_____
2. Although ideas may differ markedly, I reflect mutual respect for those communicated by all participants.	_____	_____	_____
3. The worth of the individual is of primary concern despite the wide range of differences.	_____	_____	_____
4. Good personal relations is demonstrated by word and action daily.	_____	_____	_____

- try to perceive reasonableness in the situation from the standpoint of the other person.
- when readily accepting a challenge, don't hold yourself up to be something you're not. Remember, there may be a fine line between what you really are and what you think you are. Stay within the parameters of what you are qualified and competent to do.
- don't volunteer or assume duty beyond your level of competency.
- recognize that the standard of care may change in the same activity, within the same time frame, as the risk increase and be ready to meet the change with a comparable intensity in the standard of care.
- document changes in activity and the commensurate action when an injury occurs.

- familiarize yourself and/or staff with actions which would result in the establishment of an appropriate amount of prudence for example:
  a. Conducts regular inspection of all equipment.
  b. Insists on prompt and full repair of faulty equipment.
  c. Injured are treated by those professionally prepared and certified to do so.
  d. Medical approach is necessary for participation, and return to activity following serious injury or illness.
  e. Instructional and supervisory duties are assigned to those qualified for the particular activity.
  f. Enthusiasm for accomplishment is not allowed to suppress rational behavior.

- recognize behavior which could be negligent (Harper): an act not properly done; appropriate care not employed; or the circumstance under which it is done creates risk, creates situations which are unreasonably dangerous to others. For example:
  Entrusts dangerous devices or instruments to persons who are incompetent to use or care for such instruments.
  Fails to give adequate warning or employ due care.
  Fails to employ appropriate skills to perform acts undertaken.
- conduct seminars or inservice activities to inform staff on the school law with respect to liability, negligence, tort and statutes applicable to teachers and coaches.
- explore duty and accountability through "matched pairs" or other technique(s) periodically.
- show reasonable care in the performance of voluntarily assumed duties.
- a public relations program to change the image of the teacher-coach and programs should be regularly and consistently presented.
  It should not be crisis oriented.
  What is it being sold?
  What is the attitude of the public to what is being sold?
  What is the media for selling the product or concept?
  Plan and implement the action.
  How effective was it and how could it have been more effective?

Selected References

Alexander, K., Solomon, E., *College and University Law,* Michie and Co., pp. 596-598.

Alexander, Ruth, Alexander, Kern, *Teachers and Torts,* Maxwell Publishing Co., 1970, pp. 13-22.

38 *Am. Jur.* 45-47.

_____, *Analysis of Accidents to Pupils and Employees,* Los Angeles, California, 1956, p. 21.

Appenzeller, H. and Appenzeller, T., *Sports and the Courts,* Michie Company, Charlotteville, VA, p. 16.

Asher, Mark, "Use of Drugs by Chargers Under Probe," *The Washington Post,* Sunday, May 22, 1973, p. D 1.

Danhoff v. Osborne, Circuit Court of Appeal.

Delon, F.G. "Tort Liability," *Yearbook of School Law,* 1977, pp. 70-93; *Shannon v. Addison Trail,* 339 N.E. 2d 372.

Garber, Lee O., "The Case of the Negligent Coach," *The Nations' Schools,* No. 59, May, 1959, p. 78.

Garrison, C., "Have You Acted Negligently Today?", *Athletic Journal,* No. 39, December, 1958, p. 10.

Gowen, Thomas, "Sports Programs and Injuries: Liability Since Rutter," *Pennsylvania Law Journal Reporter,* April 5, 1982, Vol. V, No. 13, pp. 2-10.

Harper, Flower V., *A Treatise on the Law of Sports,* Bobbs-Merrill Co., Indianapolis, 1938, pp. 171.

Holliday, Bob, "Court Negligence Ruling Could Alter Insurance," *The Daily Pantagraph,* Wednesday, April 22, 1981.

Hurt, Thomas W., "Elements of Tort Liability as Applied to Athletic Injuries," *The Journal of School Health,* April 1976, Vol. XLVI, No. 4, pp. 200-202.

Mallois, H.C. "The Physical Educator and the Law," *The Physical Educator,* May, 1975, Vol. 32, p. 61.

National Tort Law Digests, Goetzman v. Wichern, Washington, D.C., 1983, p. 50.

Prosser, William, *Law of Torts,* Mann Publishing, Cleveland, Ohio. 1963, p. 2.

Silance, Luc Maitre, "Sport and the Law," *News,* General Association of International Sports Federations, No. 7, July 1986, p. 2.

Ware, Martha, "Is the Teacher Liable?" *National Education Association Journal,* 47: 603, December, 1958.

CHAPTER IV
Philosophy, Rules and Dress Code

Philosophy

It is generally recognized that human movement in the form of physical activities, especially play, can be of value to the participant. Fitness, rehabilitations, health maintenance, skill development and pure pleasure have been the basis for some people to participate in a play experience. Pure play in the form of spontaneous activity for pleasure has been theorized to be a part of every segment of society (Huizinga). The pure form may be structured into a process where specific rules, time segments, and skills can be identified by all who participate in a game with an expected norm of behavior.

Physical education, sport and athletics maintain that play in a structured process affords special opportunities to teach and educate the child. Educators, philosophers, and behavioral psychologists support the position of learning through movement: athletic programs provide a unique form for the development of discipline, individual sacrifice and team work not available in other school programs (JOHPER, June 1970, Vol. 41). The changing nature of play from a pure unstructured form to a structured process and a process enhanced with competition has resulted in some problems.

The changing nature of play has been described or likened to a battlefield. "The NFL has substituted the morality of the battlefield for that of the playing field and the constraints of civilization have been left on the sidelines." (Peterson: 20)

Serious questions have been raised regarding the philosophy of school sports, the qualifications of coaches and the sensibility of popular coaching techniques (Godek:16). And, a degree of risk is a realistic part of athletics (Godek:18). However, the frequency of accident and injury is very high. Mallois reports a recent investigation disclosed 552,000 accidents reported during a one year period, and that over ½ of all injuries were those which involved physical education. (Mallois:62).

There are data which indicate that a philosophy of athletics

27

which places the good of the athletes above all other concerns and implements policies which reflect such philosophy will then have a program that is likely to be judged positively. (Godek: 16-23). To take this another step further, philosophies for programs in physical education should also place the welfare of the student above other concerns. Corresponding policies should reflect such an approach.

Rules

A parallel exists between the needs for law in society (simple to complex societies) and the need for rules in play (pure play to athletics). In pure play the rules and dimensions are usually simple, few in number, readily structured, utilized, discarded and possibly never used again. However, the play process when structured requires consistent rules, widely known, applicable to all participants, interpretation, modification, and a mode of longevity to maintain the game in its form. The addition of competition to the game, or structured process, to form athletics has made the rules more complex by layering organizational rules (NCAA, High School Association, etc.) on the process. Therefore, play in the pure form may have few rules; whereas, play as an institutionalized process requires more rules.

The discipline of physical education and sport are certainly rules oriented. Rules are an essential part of play, games, contests, athletics and sport. The professional (teacher/coach) must relate to rules in a wide variety of circumstances: "Those associated with athletics realize that rules play a vital role in sports. All matters relating to the teaching of skills and the ways in which practice sessions are conducted are to a significant degree determined by the rules of the game." (Godek:19). Although this statement focuses on athletics, it is also applicable to physical education and the teaching of sport activity in general.

Rules and authority are interrelated. "The best rules that man ever developed are no good unless they are enforced." (JOHPER: 1970) And, law is not law unless enforcement in predictable, the parallel between these two statements should be familiar. Regardless, the implication is that someone must do the enforcing. Therefore, law has granted some right to act to someone. In this case it is the teachers and coaches who have the right to act, or may have the right to act. They have been said to act in Loco Parentis (in place of parent). Authority grows out of loco parentis. (Vacca: 235-240). Administratively, the institutional right to act or perform in a particular manner is authority. And, the right to act, or who has the right to act in a particular circumstance, has been tested often, especially during the 1960's.

The troubled times of the 1960's are a prime example of social issues and the authority related to those issues being tested: environment, pollution, nuclear power, Vietnam War and student's rights. The student's rights movement became a lever for testing authority, especially in reference to the regulations of student appearance. (Vacca:235) In part, it was a search for reasonableness in relationship to some of the rules being stressed. Authority to act must be reasonable and with some restraint. Vacca states this in another way, ". . . restrictions on athletic competition must pass a 'rational relationship' test. That is, if a rule has some reasonable and rational relationship to the desired end sought by the enactment of the rule, it will likely be upheld." (Vacca:206) Significant is the *reasonable and rational relationship to the desired end.*

Reasonable and rational relationships also have a bearing on the risk in a sporting event or activity. The mere occurrence of an injury does not result in liability. However, players are expected to play within the rules. (Gowen:10). There is a norm of expected behavior, reasonable behavior, set within the framework of the rules. Or, the participant is expected to play in a particular manner. There is or should be a rational relationship between behavior set by the rules and the performance by the participant. It is when the teacher or coach modifies the rules or devises drills and exercises which are substantially outside of the normal rules of activity that problems and/or conflict develops.

Although risks persist in activity (play, games, athletics and sport), there are attempts to structure activity to the benefit of all concerned. The Congressional hearing on violence in sport is an example of such an effort. Accordingly, Phillip H. Corboy says, "litigation produces safer activity." And, there are pedagological techniques for maximizing safe participation: homogeneous grouping, medical screening, qualified teacher-coaches, proper facilities and equipment, activity counseling. SCAM is a New York state program initiated in 1975 to help participants with activity selection. The term (SCAM) stands for Selection Classification Age Maturity program. It strives to reduce injury among young athletes by identifying those who are competing in the "wrong" sport or who are physically superior or inferior...then channeling them to the most appropriate sports and levels. (Peterson:12) And, one form of injury causing conduct...difficult to weed out...is that of negligent instruction of the fundamentals of a sport.

(Peterson:20) Instruction in rules of performance and fair play would have to fall into this category: (T)his court believes that when athletes are engaged in an athletic competition: all teams involved are trained and coached by knowledgeable personnel; a recognized set of rules governs the conduct of the competitions; and a safety rule is contained therein which is primarily designed to protect players from serious injury, a player is then charged with a legal duty to every other player on the field to refrain from conduct proscribed by a safety rule." (Peterson:13)

Basically, rules exist in sport and activity; they simply imply authority to act; they set a pattern of expected behavior or reasonable performance, although risks exist.

Dress Codes

An area of primary concern for coaches and teachers in physical education and sport has been performance and appearance. In some instances there has been a pre-occupation with the relationship between the two. Television and radio commercials have sounded the LOOK sharp, FEEL sharp, BE sharp message to all viewers and listeners. Akin to a "look sharp, play sharp" syndrome, professionals have also made or inferred a connection with self-discipline. Irrespective of the rationale, a natural relationship has been the establishment of appearance codes, dress codes or training rules and regulations. The views on this topic have been divergent, especially with regard to "morale" and affected by enforcement of such rules. However, many coaches considered enforcement of such regulations a legitimate means of building team morale, discipline and team spirit. (JOHPER: 1970) Because of the perceived need for such dress code and rules of appearance, they have been widely implemented by teachers and coaches. However, the implementation has also led to a test of authority, the authority to regulate student appearance. Vacca maintains that the appearance controversy followed five different routes or channels. The courts:

1) elected not to question the authority of the school personnel in effecting policies and regulations they deemed wise.
2) maintained . . . school . . . restrictions must be related to the enforcement of public service.
3) stated . . . Loco Parentis does not clothe school authorities . . . absolute control . . . parents also share in such matters as grooming . . . discipline for the sake of discipline and uniformity is inconsistent with the melting pot idea.

4) reflected . . . conflicting opinion . . . but rules insure safety.
5) reflected . . . a growing reluctance. (Vacca:236-238)

Despite a variety of responses to this social conflict, a real danger does exist. The real danger in this test of authority is the deterioration of value, or hesitancy of teachers or coaches in teaching values. The question becomes, what type of dress code or rules of appearance is reasonable if we are to take advantage of our uniqueness and teach such values as self-discipline, individual sacrifice, teamwork or morale? There are components to consider when trying to establish dress codes or rules:

1. *The rule or code should represent a consensus effort* directed to a specific end. Those involved with the problem should help establish the code: teacher administrator, student and parent. It should not be mere *IPSE DIXIT* (a dogmatic assertion made on authority but not proven), a person or committee seeking to impose discipline for the sake of discipline and conformity alone, (Richards V. Thurston, 304 F. Supp. 449, 454).

2. *The rule must pass a "rational relationship" test.* That is, if a rule has some reasonable or rational relationship to the desired end sought by the enactment of the rule, it will likely be upheld. (Vacca:205-214) . . . rules concerning dress, appearance and off-campus conduct of athletes must shoulder burden of proof that they have substantial relationship to fitness for competition, (Bunger V. Iowa High School Ath. Assoc.; 197 N.W. 2d 555).

3. *The purpose(s) or end(s) of such a rule or rules should be clearly identified* and reasonable in relationship to the rule. They should be measureable and justifiable as compared to mere whims. What is implied is that planning and thought is as essential to teaching a value as to teaching the activity skill.

4. *A philosophical basis of the rule or code could be expressed in a preamble* which would focus on instilling specific qualities in team members through the activity and the values of athletes and physical education in total education. (JOHPER: 1970).

The Legal Council, California Teachers Association, provides an excellent format for dress codes or rules in the June 1970 issue of the "Journal of Health, Physical Education, and Recreation:"

First . . . important that the purpose tends to inculcate in the pupil principles of justice, fair play, good sportsmanship, good citizenship and respect for rules and authority. The coach needs to establish that his purpose is to instill these qualities in team members through athletics.

Second, the value of athletics in total education of the student must be stated. Competitive sports sharpens intellect, improve concentration, help assure that a healthy body is going to be able to do better mental work.

These two philosophical cornerstones for the preamble of a rule which might read, "In order to inculcate good sportsmanship, respect for rules and authority, establish leadership, team pride, team work, team discipline, as well as eliminate disruptive influences, disturbances in the lockerroom, on the training field, on the playing field, on trips and off school grounds. The following rules are established:" (JOHPER, June 1970, Vol. 41).

Summary

- Physical activity, especially athletics, provides a unique form for the development of discipline, individual sacrifice and team work not available in other school programs.
- A degree of risk is a realistic part of athletics, sport and physical education.
- Litigation has raised questions about the philosophy of school sports, qualification of coaches, and the sensibility of their techniques.
- Program philosophies which reflect the welfare of the student above other concerns are viewed positive.
- Physical education, sport and athletics are rules oriented.
- Rules are dependent upon enforcement for effectiveness and authority is an implied action.
- Authority or the right to act has been regularly tested.
- Rules must be reasonable and bear a rational relationship to a desired end.
- Risk can be minimized through a variety of techniques.
- A reasonable form of behavior is set within the framework of the rules.
- Dress codes and rules are an attempt to teach values.
- The teaching of values demands deliberate and systematic planning.
- Rules should represent a consensus of effort.
- Purposes or ends should be clearly identified.

You're in Their Shoes

1. All athletes shall be clean shaven, free of moustaches, with sideburns trimmed no lower than earlobe level, and hair trimmed and well groomed. The hair in the back will not extend below the top of an ordinary shirt collar and on the sides, the hair shall not extend below earlobe level.
   - Is the rule reasonable in relationship to a desired end?
2. All athletes will have their hair well trimmed, well groomed, and it will not extend below the top of an ordinary shirt collar. This or other grooming may be necessary to facilitate helmet fits and safety.
   - Does a duty exist to provide safe equipment standards?
   - Is there a rational relationship between the rule and a desired end?
3. While conducting class, a student enters to participate with hair dyed purple, and the student is subsequently sent to the office. The student was banned for having purple hair after the principal decided that school wasn't the place for multicolored hair.
   - Is there a need to define relationships as a result of social change?
   - Was the action reasonable?
   - Does a rational relationship exist with the implied purpose?

Risk Management Suggestions

- It is a considered good management technique to develop a policy manual. Such a manual should contain philosophical position statements which are professionally sound and reflects on the welfare of the student.
- It is necessary to identify and differentiate between rules, policy and guidelines.
- Modify activities to reduce risk and not produce risk.
- Identify the desired result or end before establishing a rule.
- Utilize consensus effort to establish a rule and study the relationship between the rule and the desired end.
- A central purpose of training rules and dress codes should be the development of a positive sport safety attitude.

CHAPTER V
Injury

A significant data base exists to confirm the active nature of Americans. Sports safety data reflects that 90% of Americans participate in at least 1 of 75 different sports. (Yost: 7) Additionally, the President's Council on Physical Fitness and Sport recently reported that 53% of the U.S. population is in strong exercise daily. (PCPFS, November 1982)

The wide variety of sporting events on television bares witness to the popularity of sport and physical activity by the millions of viewers. These viewers come to expect injury as part of the sports scene as athletes try to best the efforts of their opponents. Peterson presents some interesting data:

- Each year sports causes over 17 million injuries that require medical attention.
- Over one million high school football players in 20,000 schools and 70,000 college players at 900 colleges are injured . . .
- 86% of all high school players will sustain one injury in their career.
- 1933 to 1976 organized football claimed 1,198 lives with over half between ages of 16 and 18. (Peterson: 10-20)

Although risks persist in activity, injury is a very real expectation in sport. When a young man goes out for sports, he has a 50/50 chance of injury. (Yost: 6) And, the injury phenomena has had a devastating effect on education and business. Without a discussion on the pros and cons of the circumstances, the fate of the trampoline in gymnastics is common knowledge. California schools in 1978 reported a 300% increase in the cost of liability insurance. (Peterson: 10) Gymnastics and football are two sports whose support industries have had stressful economic times, especially the football helmet manufacturer.

In 1978 helmet (FB) manufacturers faced $116 to $150 million dollars in pending law suits on their products. (Peterson: 10) This represented 5 to 6 times the industry's annual gross sales of $24 million and 100 times its annual profits. (Peterson: 10) The result was a reduction in the number of manufactures.

A first step in combatting the injury phenomena in sports and physical education is to expect that injuries can be reduced, not necessarily eliminated. It is an attitude problem. If accidents/injuries just happen and are uncontrollable, then there is nothing that can be done. However, if accidents are caused, then factors can be controlled or regulated to affect the cause and reduce the frequency of accidents or the chance of accidents. If risk is expected, then something can be done to control risk. It is generally accepted that the school must provide a safe play environment. This would certainly help in managing risk. Next, schools must be certain that risk is kept at an acceptable level. (Godek: 18) The professional can raise questions and seek answers which will minimize risk and keep it at an acceptable level. Godek, J. in "Prevention and Management of Sports Injuries" provides a meaningful list for consideration. His eleven factors can also be elaborated upon:

1. Is the medical examination required for sports participation adequate? (Godek: 18)

   The specialist in physical education or sports should be aware of the health status of the participant. A certain body of knowledge should be available to allow for planning to meet the needs of the participant within certain parameters. Guidelines for the medical examination have been expressed in sports safety and sports medicine materials. (Craig, T., *Current Sports Medicine Issues*, AAHPE Publication, Washington, D.C., 1974)

   It is suggested that the type of information needed comes from an examination focusing on four areas: blood, urinalysis, medical history, and special problems. R. Lane in "Medical Basis of Restriction from Athletics" states it as follows:

   ". . . to determine proper sports placement for an individual . . . physician . . . to administer a medical screening exam . . . should consist of the following basics:

   1. A complete medical history, with special attention to factors important to the sport in question.
   2. A complete, specially directive physical examination.
   3. A complete blood count.
   4. A urinalysis."

   The dual purposes of the medical examination should be kept in mind. It functions not only to identify what activities should be ruled out, but also to target what activities can be participated in. And, the professional teacher/coach should be cognizant of the health status parameters needed for the activity by the participant(s). It may be necessary for the activity specialist to provide a sport medical history, or seek this information in order to insure articulation of activity and participant condition. Health status is a meaningful variable to and an overriding consideration in physical activity (play, sport, athletics).

2. Is there a policy that requires administration of some test to assess an acceptable level of physical fitness relative to the demands of his/her sport? (Godek: 18)

    Basically, it implies that the condition of the human machine relative to the activity should be known before the activity is started. It should not be happenchance; but planned for and insured by policy.

3. Is all equipment safe? (Godek: 18)

4. Does the equipment meet all acceptable standards of performance? (Godek: 18)

    The positive aspect of product liability has been the establishment of performance standards by some manufactures with accompanying labels, tags, and guidelines. It pays for the teacher/coach to seek such information and standards.

5. Has every precaution been taken to make the play environment safe? (Godek: 18)

    The old axiom of "never play where you haven't checked" certainly fits into establishing a safe play environment: basketball coach looking for moisture on the floor; a play field being checked for gopher holes or foreign objects by the physical education teacher.

6. Do coaches . . . know where . . . combination of heat and humidity presents a health hazard, . . . how to modify activity . . . when to cancel . . . and is there school policy? (Godek: 18)

7. Are proper skills taught and practiced regularly? (Godek: 18)

8. Are practice sessions and competitions conducted with previous arrangements for health care delivery? (Godek: 19)

    It should be understood that health care items are not solely the concern of the coach and athletics. Physical education teachers should also relate to the heat/humidity hazard, modification of activity, proper skills, health care delivery and related school policy.

9. Does the school have a medically approved and verified proce-

dure for determining proper weight class for wrestlers? (Godek: 18)

Individuals close to the sport of wrestling know of situations where extreme weight cuts have occurred. The fact that they may have been ill-advised or not advised creates a risk to the participant. The weight reduction phenomena in wrestling has been a persistent problem confronted by state high school athletic association, wrestling rules committees and wrestling coaches. Abuses in this area can be controlled by a medically approved policy, common sense and good judgement.

10. Does the school have specific policy regarding handling of athletic injuries? (Godek: 19)
   a. Does every team have a specific plan for dealing with injuries?
   b. Is a telephone readily accessible?

It should be recognized that the force, speed and movement component of each sport tends to foster a pattern of common injuries. The "hit or be hit" nature of football gives rise to concussions, broken bones, bad knees, neck injuries not common to tennis or swimming. Therefore, specificity of details for sport, injury and care must vary from sport to sport.

Additionally, the fact that some activity sites may be outside and several fields away from a building and phone may raise a question of accessibility, especially when the accident is critical, catastrophic and demands immediate response.

11. Is there a policy regarding the qualifications of coaches? (Godek: 19)

This may be examined in another way. Where teacher competency is in question or absent, the board, district or administrator may have a responsibility to adopt and enforce rules for activity, stating what should or should not be done by the teacher-coach.

Injury to the student-athlete must be recognized as a leading cause of litigation. *Welch v. Dunsmuir,* the coach failed to properly supervise removal of the injured student. (Enos: 10) Certain questions could have been asked which did not require medical training but would have given indication as to the nature of the injury. "Doctor, in determining just what did damage to the spinal cord, is movement of the fingers, hands, and feet the most significant thing?" He testified, "Actually far more important than any kind of examination that one can make of the local injury." (Welch v. Dunsmuir, 326 p. 2d 633)

Pirkle v. Oakdale, 253 p. 2d 1, a question was raised about the delay in getting medical aid to the injured party aggravated the injury.

An extensive list of injuries and circumstances could easily be developed. Regardless, another essential step in risk control is recognizing what situations are most likely to result in conflict or problems which could lead to a liability litigation. Three situations have been identified by Godek, J., which bear consideration: (Godek: 17)

1. *Prior to An Injury*: Was everything done to prevent (the injury)?
2. *At the Time of the Injury*: Did the athlete receive care that was correct and acceptable?
3. *Returning a previously injured athlete to participation*: Was the athlete adequately recovered or did return to activity aggravate an existing condition or predispose the athlete to some other problem?

These questions might give rise to the inquiry about the standard of care exercised in each circumstance:

Prior to injury: Medical examination, teaching of proper skills, teaching of rules, proper equipment, nature of facility, conduct of the activity, etc.

At time of Injury: First aid, emergency care, accessibility of phone, type of medical care and follow up, policies and procedures for emergencies, transportation, etc.

Returning to Participation: Release to activity, prognosis for involvement, recordkeeping, monitoring and follow up, matching skill levels, post injury check up, readiness to return, etc.

The standard of care requires the anticipation of a wide range of dangerous acts and conditions which could expose the student to unreasonable risk of harm. (Enos: 11) Recovery has been *permitted where injury resulted from overcrowded conditions or the equipment was defective; also, when injured while performing a particular exercise under the direction of teacher, particularly when student protested or indication student was not prepared or was not properly instructed . . .*

Frequently recovery has been denied when:

1. The game was not essentially dangerous.
2. Nothing was wrong with the equipment or premise.

3. The exercise was simple and injury could not have been anticipated.
4. The equipment was in proper condition and used by the regular P.E. class.
5. The injury occurred as a result of an unavoidable collision and the game was not essentially hazardous. (Enos: 9)

Summary

- Pupil injury is a leading cause of liability litigation, and it has had a dramatic impact on education and business.
- For the most part accidents are caused, and there are related factors which can be controlled or regulated to help reduce the frequency level of accidents.
- Questions can be raised by the teacher-coach about the medical examination, fitness level, equipment/standards, play environment, activity methods, proper skills, emergency procedures, qualifications, and specific sport needs or problems, the answers to which would help reduce risk.
- Problem areas related to injury involve what was done prior to injury, at the time of injury, and upon return to participation.
- Standard of care requires the anticipation or forseeability of a wide range of acts, situations and conditions which would expose the student-athlete to a wide range of unreasonable risk.
- The range of questions and guidelines are applicable to all professionals who deal with physical activity not only the coach and athletes. Health status of the participant is a meaningful variable in physical education and leisure pursuits. And, the factors of emergency care, accessibility of telephone, proper instruction, activity modification, etc. must be professional concerns of the teacher in physical or other supervision of play activity.
- Accident and injury can be complicated in definition and understanding by social attitudes, social roles, and social expectations.

You're In Their Shoes

1. Practice in your sport has been intensive, grueling and physically demanding for most of the week. As a result of the routine and equipment slippage, your blue chip performer developed several blisters. And, it is evident during early part of the scheduled competition that his performance is below par and some movements affected.
   - What parameters exist between the performance and physical

40

condition which establishes an injury?
- Does the teacher-coach have a duty to raise questions and modify activity to minimize risk of injury?

2. During your activity class a student was kicked in the stomach, you asked the student to lie down, be inactive, and covered her with a blanket. Two hours later, after the student passed urine containing blood, you rushed her home and sought medical treatment.
   - Could a layman (reasonably) be expected to discover the nature of the injury sooner?

3. A player has a history of shoulder separations. While practicing after having clearance from a doctor, the player again separates the shoulder. You and the player corrected the injury and put the arm into a sling. The player dressed, went home, attended school regularly, and did not seek medical treatment.
   - Did the coach breach a duty to render or seek medical aid?

Risk Management Suggestions

- develop procedures for gathering information about the health status of individuals before they participate and employ modifications as indicated.
- develop skill in assessing and interpreting the information provided by a medical examination and where necessary, request additional information in relationship to the essentials of a good medical examination.
- develop procedures and policies for handling medical emergencies in physical education and athletics.
- examine the accessibility of telephones to distant play fields. The cordless and rechargeable technology has made it economically feasible in most instances.
- develop a comprehensive injury reporting system to include data prior to injury, at time of injury, during treatment, and upon return to activity.
- utilize reporting system to identify frequency of particular accidents, identify causal factors and implement steps to reduce risks.
- develop a system for inspection and assessment of facilities and equipment.
- seek out equipment with standards of performance parallel to or greater than the needs of the activity and the level of the performer.

- consider the adaptation of a safety model which encourages the teacher-coach to identify risk or hazards, remove risks/hazards where possible, compensate where risks/hazards cannot be removed, and create no additional risks/hazards.
- modify activity to the benefit of the participant: reduce overcrowding, form ability groups, effective time management, etc. Modify to reduce risks not produce risks.
- remember that the health of the participant is the meaningful variable and overriding consideration in all activity.

Selected References

Enos, Donald F., *Supervision: Who's Responsible for the Law and the Irresponsible Somebody*, U.S. Dept. of HEW, March 1975, pp. 1-15.

Godek, J. "Prevention and Management of Sports Injuries—Questions About Liability," *NASSP*, Sept. 1981, pp. 16-23.

Peterson, T.L., and Smith, Scott, "The Role of the Lawyer on the Playing Field," *Barrister*, pp. 10-13 and 20.

Welch v. Dunsmuir, 326 p. 2d 633.

Yost, P., *Sport Safety*, NEA, AAHPERD—Division of Safety, Washington, D.C., 1973, p.6.

CHAPTER VI
Violence

Virtually any sport participant, especially the athlete, can attest to slogans and motivational urgings which imply or suggest extremes in the use of force: "attack," "take him out," "no pain, no gain," "give yourself up for the ball," "no guts," "stick'em," to mention a few. And, although the urgings are intended to produce assertiveness, aggressiveness, intensity or the extra effort needed for achieving success, it often results in the interpretation that "winning" is the only thing and anything goes to gain it.

The wide panorama of sport available to the American public is often viewed in a narrow sense. It is viewed that "Winning at all cost" is peculiar to American society and violence is its close relative. Recently, an international authority, Dr. Pierre Seurin, provided a perspective on this problem. Dr. Seurin maintained that certain things are true of competitive sports for all countries:

> "Victory at all costs is the only thing that counts: the essential thing is to win, even if it means resorting to cheating, rough play, and the danger of doping: to win means competing aggressively, not to say ferociously; this decisive psychological factor is increasingly taken into account by trainers and competitors, and to acquire it, lengthy specialized training is necessary. For many athletes this increasingly demanding type of training is time-consuming (several hours a day) leaving little leisure or energy for other cultural activities, or even for normal professional activities and family life. There is also unfortunately the exploitation—of gifted young children who are forced to undergo a very hard training at an early age, the physiological and psychological dangers of which have been pointed out by both doctors and educators." (Seurin: 1983)

(Dr. Pierre Seurin, now deceased, was the President and leader of Federation International d'Education Physique, scholar and world traveler).

Further evidence of the global nature of this problem and phenomena is not hard to find. An old adage in an Australian contact sport, rugby, proclaims "if you can't take it—don't play it," (Queensland Law Society Journal). A member of the Welsh Rugby Union team 1978 made this observation despite his broken jaw and impaired speech, "you give some, you get some." (Queensland Law Society Journal) His jaw fractured by a right cross thrown in the heat of the game.

One need only recall the 1985 soccer game between England and Belgium which resulted in violence, death and an international incident to be current with the time.

Violence and the "Win at all cost" syndrome are viewed as being interrelated. The "Win at all cost" philosophy creates an atmosphere where undue violence . . . is likely to occur. (Woolf: 1) Any spectator can verify the expected behavior in many sports. The baseball manager is expected to belly-up to the umpire and kick dirt, or he is viewed as something less than effective. Hockey players are expected to "battle on the boards." One of the first cases in sports violence occurred on September 21, 1969. Boston Bruin, Ted Green, almost lost his life when struck by a hockey stick wielded by Wayne Maki of St. Louis. (Woolf: 2) And, the defensive back in football is to intimidate receivers to the point of distraction. At one time, the "clothesline" technique was good intimidation, producing many injuries. A coaching technique was to make the receiver shy or lose concentration by focusing on the "patter of little feet."

Irrespective of the act producing violent sport intimidation, violence tarnishes the image of both sport and society. Whether on the play fields, in professional sport or in the Olympics, society and sport both suffer:

> The game (football) became contaminated, but the process was so gradual and so insidious that few took notice. From the kiddie leagues to the major colleges and professional leagues, the sport's public image grew more robust even as it decayed within. The injury rate mounted, sportsmanship declined. Vicious acts became commonplace. (Rains: 797)

Although the process described hints at social evolution, the professional (teacher-coach) in sport would also relate to the fact that youth will seek "role" models and emulate. There must be a "trickle down" affect from the professional ranks to colleges and then to the "kiddies," regardless of their team affiliation.

The violence of Kermit Washington against Rudy Tomjanovich during a professional basketball game resulted in a $3.3 million dollar award for injuries inflicted (fractured skull, jaw, nose and other facial injuries). (Woolf: 3) Washington acted . . . reckless disregard for safety of others. (Woolf: 3) Additionally, while the Steelers' Terry Bradshaw was completing a páss to Franco Harris in a game between the Pittsburgh Steelers and Oakland Raiders, some distance away the Raiders' George Atkinson rushed up behind an unsuspecting Lynn Swan and hit him with his forearm at the base of the helmet. (Rains: 796) Swan became a casualty of the game. Whether it is basketball, football, or the enforcer in hockey, violence in professional sports has been a social concern, resulting in congressional investigation. James Michener in *Sports in America* maintains that American sport reflects the inherent violence of our society. And, litigation has been one manner of regulating violence in sport. This is clearly pointed out in Hackbart v. Cincinnati Bengals, where Judge William Doyle made some observations:

> Booby Clark had a pass thrown to him . . . It was intercepted . . . he was illegally blocked by Hackbart . . . he hit Hackbart on the back of the head with his forearm while Hackbart was on one knee . . . serious neck fracture. Blow served on legitimate purpose. (435 F. Supp. 352) (Woolf: 2) Clark's act . . . was intentional . . . strictly prohibited by rules (NFL) . . . not inherent to the game. (Woolf: 3)

> The 10th U.S. Circuit Court transmitted this sobering message to the sports establishment—if they cannot keep their house clean, the courts will not hesitate to do it for them. (Rains: 803)

Cameron Rains has reflected on the impact of some of the recent cases. The Nabozny v. Barnhill case emphasis was made on control, "(W)e also believe that organized athletic competition must accompany every athlete onto the playing field," (Rains: 801) The restraints imply control. Wherein does the control of sport and violence rest? Traditionally, sports violence has been controlled by means of game penalties, fines, and suspensions. (Rains: 797) It has been suggested that the internal administrator's close contact with the development of the game and its players better enable him to regulate the level of violence. (Rains: 797)

Although these opinions were made in relationship to professional sports, one can apply them to the sports scene in schools, especially physical education and athletics. The question could be raised, "if the teacher and or coach is the immediate administrator, does he/she know better than anyone what conduct is

45

reasonable and what risks the players assume?" Additionally, the question would develop as to whether or not an official is part of the administrative network. Regardless of the answer, it should be recognized that the official is instrumental in regulation of the game within the framework of the rules. The court held that in competitive sports in which 1) the competitors are trained and coached by knowledgeable personnel; 2) a recognized set of rules governs the conduct of the competition; and 3) safety rules are contained therein which are designed to protect players from serious injury; the standard of care owed . . . is "to refrain from conduct proscribed by a safety rule." (Rains: 801, 334 N.E. 2d 258)

Despite the numerous litigations, the courts have exercised restraint, and a reluctance toward being a smothering effect on sport. They have recognized the contribution of sport to society in various opinions, "Many valuable lessons are learned in athletics, among them leadership, pride, hard work, cooperation and sportsmanship. Society should not, and cannot, tolerate the erosion of these benefits by allowing unrestrained violence, which benefits no one and injures many." (Rains: 802)

The benefits of physical activity, sport and athletics can only be achieved if the professional in those disciplines address the problems of the "Win at all cost" syndrome and violence in activity.

Summary

- Violence is a very real social aspect of sport, global in nature, and related to the "Win at all Cost" approach cultivated by *some* teachers-coaches.
- Violence, whether by social evolution or the emulating of role models exists at all levels of play: youth leagues, schools, colleges, professional sports and international competition.
- Violence has a diminishing and sobering affect on the expressed values of sport and activity: self-discipline, leadership, teamwork, pride, hardwork, fair play, and sportsmanship become tarnished and lose perspective when violence occurs.
- Violence, in some instance, is not clearly separable from the assertive, aggressive or extra effort essential for achievement in sport.
- Violence, the intent to do harm, should not be condoned but is encouraged by some motivational techniques or urgings in performance.
- Violence, as viewed by the courts, can be controlled by some internal administrative efforts.

- Violence is encouraged through spectators who expect certain forms of behavior beyond the normal components of the game.
- One form of sport violence is the reckless disregard for the safety of others, resulting in harm or injury.
- The professional in physical education, sport and athletics must accept the responsibility for controlling violence in sport or face the obvious, litigation and the courts will control sport and activity.
- The professional teacher-coach should be capable of identifying reasonable conduct and the risks natural to the activity.
- The responsibility for the control of violence should rest with the player, parent, spectator, coach, official and administrator. All of these people have a role to play in answering responsible performance.
- Rules of a sport govern the conduct of competition and establish a safety code to protect the participant from injury.
- The court and legal opinion have recognized the values of athletics: leadership, pride, hard work, cooperation, sportsmanship.
- Society should not allow the erosion of these benefits by allowing violence in sport to be unchecked at any level of performance.

You're In Their Shoes

1. The basketball game is well into the second half, and although it is not a runaway, the momentum of the game and score is to your favor. Your center and the opposition's center have moved from assertive bumps for position, to aggressive elbowing and a hard shove away from the action with no penalty. These same two teams scuffled at mid-court during an away game early in the season.
   - Is it the officials' responsibility to regulate conformity to the rules of the game, at this point?
   - Is the action a natural part of basketball?
   - Does an early season incident indicate a need for present planning and controls to prevent an outbreak reoccurring?

2. While checking facilities, you overhear the baseball coach chiding his team to take the defensive player out on a slide, sharpening cleats and doing it any way possible.
   - Is coaching philosophy and technique solely the responsibility of the individual?

3. Prior to the start of the football game a pep rally is held to cheer and motivate the team against its crosstown rival. Even

47

more significant was the team rally prior to going on the field. While in a tight circle and shouting at fever pitch, a gold painted chicken was tossed into the middle and stomped to death. The demise of the representative "golden eagle" had only a fleeting influence. Despite scoring first and quickly, the rivals won big.

• Are motivational gimmicks, such as the above, rational techniques for student development?

• Do sport and society both suffer from such questionable techniques?

• What duty does an administrator have when personnel exercise poor judgment in motivating performers?

Risk Management Suggestions

• Develop and establish a philosophy toward sport activity which places the welfare of the student first. Periodic seminars with staff, personnel, assistant coaches, or the students in the program should strive for consensus and consistency toward winning and other programmatic matters.

• Examine the use of motivational terminology or techniques which urge or support the "win at all cost" concept.

• A clear distinction should be made between assertive or aggressive behavior essential to the sporting effort and violence which is the intent to do harm or injury.

• Behavior which reflects intentional infliction of injury should not be condoned.

• Behavior which reflects the reckless disregard for the safety of others should not be condoned.

• Students with a history of over aggressive behavior patterns would be identified, monitored and possibly restricted from competitive activities.

• A positive sport safety attitude should be an essential objective in program planning, a regard for the safety of others.

• Consider the use of small discussion groups or encounter groups to help in the resolution of violent incidents occurring in the sport setting.

Selected References

Hackbart v. Cincinnati Bengals, 435 F. Supp. 352.
Michener, James, *Sports in America*, Random House, 1976.
Nabozny v. Barnhill, 31 Ill. App. 3rd 212, 334 N.E. 2d 258.
Rains, Cameron, Jay, "Sports Violence: A Matter of Societal Concern," *Notre Dame Lawyer*, Vol. 55, June, 1980, pp. 796-813.

Seurin, Pierre, "Sporting Life," *International Social Science Journal,* UNESCO, Vol. XXXIV, No. 2 1982, pp. 297-298.

——————— "Sport and the Law—Supreme Court Blows the Whistle," *Queensland Law Society Journal,* October, 1980, pp. 295-296.

Woolf, R., "Courts Coming Down Hard on Excessively Violent Players," *National Law Journal,* June 1980, p. 13.

CHAPTER VII
Assumption of Risk

Assumption of risk has been defined as, when a risk is knowingly and voluntarily assumed. For years the professional teacher-coach sought refuge within this meaning.

Sport activity specialist accepted as natural the implication that voluntary participation meant assuming the risks of the activity. And, even though the risks weren't known by the participant, the mere fact that they came out for the sport and donned the garb afforded the coach liberty in designing and planning practices. Often the practices were planned around the axiom of "no pain, no gain." And, for many years and in many states recovery for injury in physical activity was barred, because the participant assumed, "voluntarily," the risk of the activity.

Now, however, "assumption of risk" is under examination and new dimensions are being established. Also, the term "incurred risk" seems to be gaining popularity and support. The new dimension and terminology are a result of the reckless and tortuous conduct in sport that resulted in injury and then litigation. Generally, the cases were divided into two categories: 1) those in which the plaintiff reasonably assumed risk, and 2) those in which the plaintiff unreasonably assumed risk. (Tucker: 749) The emphasis seemed to be on the voluntary aspect of participation. More recently, as a result of numerous cases, the emphasis was placed on the "knowing and voluntary" entrance into activity risk.

> "Mere knowledge of the risk is not sufficient under the Restatement. (Restatement of Torts) The plaintiff must "appreciate the danger itself and the nature, character, and extent which makes it unreasonable," and assume the risk voluntarily. In other words, the plaintiff must voluntarily take his chances of injury, and if he is injured because of the particular risks of which he was actually aware, he cannot recover." (Tucker: 751)

The dependency on the knowing and voluntary aspect has been further altered by Nabozny v. Barnhill and Bourque v. Duplichin as reported by Tucker. Recklessness was the social behavior which helped shape some new direction in both instances:

Nabozny was a goalkeeper in a soccer game who received serious head injuries in violation of the games rules.

Bourque was injured in a collision five feet from second base in a competitive baseball game.

Accordingly, Neil Tucker points out that "violations of safety rules are actionable even if such violations are frequent and foreseeable (Nabozny); whereas, the court ruling in Bourque held:

> [a] participant in a game or sport assumes all of the risks incidental to that particular activity which are obvious and foreseeable. A participant does not assume the risk of injury from fellow players acting in an unexpected or unsportsman-like way with a reckless lack of concern for other participating. (Tucker: 754)

Mr. T.L. Gowen reported on a further examination of the voluntary assumption risk in the State of Pennsylvania, the Supreme Court questioned, "What risk can the appellant be said to have voluntarily assumed? One possibility is that he assumed the *risk of all injuries related to training for and playing football.* A second possibility is that he assumed the risk of all injuries related to *training for and playing football while under the direction of coaches who furnished watchful supervision and protective equipment when needed* . . . The court further observed the *plaintiff's voluntary act was that he associated himself with a program which was presumed to be competently and safely administered."* (Gowen: 2) It did not necessarily follow that aspiring to play the participant also assumed risk of an ancillary form of training, required by the coaches. (Gowen: 2)

A further shift away from the voluntary assumption of risk is evident from the Tomjanovich and Los Angeles Lakers case. And, although it occurred in professional athletics, the concepts and implications may have a trickle down effect on sport at other levels. As an example, Tomjanovich was struck by Laker Kermit Washington. The injury causing blow was not the common form of basketball contact. It certainly was not the contact naturally incurred in basketball, and was in violation of the rules. Significant is the difference in contact which the athlete could incur in a sport. Thomas L. Gowen elaborated further on the Tomjanovich vs. California Sports Incorporated, "aside from the obvious theories of battery, with the respondent superior component, . . . alleged . . . were negligent in failing to adequately train and supervise its employees and in retaining the services of Kermit

Washington." (Gowen: 2) A comparable action could be maintained against other sports programs given a similar set of facts in Gowen's opinion:

1. The actor causing the altercation could be primarily liable party.
2. If he is an employee acting in the scope of the employment, then the employer may be secondarily liable.
3. Whether or not an employer, the organization could be liable for failure to adequately supervise its coaches or players.
4. . . . may be liable for failure to prevent offensive conduct if it can be shown the actor has a known tendency to violence and was permitted to remain in the program.
5. Organizations may also be liable for a failure to prevent injury by active intervention of the staff in a fight involving participants. (Gowen: 2)

The comments and opinion by Thomas L. Gowen with regard to Rutter v. Northeastern Beaver School District (437 A2d 1198) have real meaning for physical education and the coach. He states that there are implications for operating sports programs:

1. . . . athletes can look to their coaches and programs not only for competent athletic instruction, but also for the judgement of the reasonably prudent person in observing safety practices, and for providing or requiring protective equipment.
2. . . . duty to competently and safely supervise recreational or competitive sports programs will vary with the sport, degree of skill of the athletes, age and experience of the participants, extent to which the athlete surrendered their own judgement to that of the coaches, and the foreseeability of injury if due care is not exercised. Sports vary as to the degree of exposure to risk of injury and the gravity of injuries that occur. (Gowen: 2)
3. Players assume risk...so long as the game is played by the rules...the mere occurrence of an injury does not give rise to liability absent negligence . . . Where coaches devise games, or exercises that do not utilize the normal rules of the game, the risks of liability may be greater under what might be . . . negligent program design theory (Gowen:10) . . . a theory that the instructor deviated from the rules of the game, created his own format for teaching and failed to exercise care for the safety of the participants. (Gowen: 10)

An early case Vendrell v. School District No. 26C, Malheur

County, 376 P. 2d 406 (1962), provides opinions which parallel and contrast the changes in the doctrine. Segments in the case report were drawn from Harper and James, *The Law of Torts and Prosser on Torts*. The voluntary aspect was supported from Harper and James.

"Voluntary participants in lawful games, sports, and even rough house, assume the risk of injury at the hands of their fellow participants (and of course of 'hurting themselves'), so long as the game is played in good faith and without negligence." (Law and Amateur Sports: 62)

Those who participate or sit as spectators at sports and amusements assume all the obvious risks of being hurt . . . was drawn from Prosser. Reference is also made to dangers inherent in the game or contest. (Law and Amateur Sport: 62). The inherent risks were expressed as those risks attendant upon being tackled. It was also mentioned that to extract the body clashes that cause bruises, jolts and hard falls would end the sport. The inherent risk in being tackled was obvious. And, finally the defendant's coaches gave the football squad adequate, standard instruction and practice. (Law and Amateur Sports: 62)

In a few years, it appears the emphasis will rest on the participant knowing what they are volunteering for, what risks are inherent to the sport, what the obvious risks are, and whether an adequate, standard of instruction was provided by the coach.

The problem is further complicated when risk is extended to include psychological and social injury along with physical injury, as in *Subjects at Risk*, 45 CFR 46, 1036:

"Means any individual who may be exposed to the possibility of injury, including physical, psychological, or social injury, as a consequence of participation as a subject in any research, development or related activity which departs from the application of those established and accepted methods necessary to meet his needs, or which increase the ordinary risks of daily life, including the recognized risks inherent in a chosen occupation or field of service."

Summary

- Assumption of risk is when a risk is knowingly and voluntarily assumed.
- Risk is any situation, circumstance or phenomena which may expose the person (student) to the possibility of injury, be it physical, psychological or social.

54

- Tortuous conduct in sport activity is affecting changes in and clarification of the assumption risk.
- Voluntary assumption of risk includes knowing and appreciating (actual awareness) the obvious dangers of the activity.
- The obvious dangers of an activity includes those risks particular to, natural to, incidental to and foreseeable in a particular activity. Specifically:
  - risk of all injuries related to training for and play a sport activity.
  - risk related to training for and playing under the direction of coaches who furnish supervision and protective equipment.
  - risk of association with a program presumed to be competently and safely administered.

- Assumption of risk may not necessarily include unexpected or unsportsmanlike action beyond that proscribed by the rules of the sport activity.
- Rules of a game, contest or activity usually proscribe conduct or behavior which a student would naturally incur through participation.
- The administration should supervise its teachers and coaches.
- A vulnerability to litigation may exist for failure to prevent offensive conduct if it can be shown that the student or athlete has a known tendency to violence and was permitted to remain in the program without supervisory action.
- The degree and level of risk will vary with the activity; the level at which the activity is presented; and, the extent to which the nature of the activity changes in its performance context in a given period of time.
- Risks may be created through negligent program design.
- Risks may be minimized through adequate and competent instruction, protective equipment, safety standards and practices, and conforming to the rules of the activity.
- Risks for the participant should be those which would be incurred naturally and obviously as a part of the activity and not those of an ancillary nature which deviate from the rules, create a different format, negate safety and condones offensive conduct.
- Risks are not limited to physical harm but may include those of a psychological and social nature.

You're In Their Shoes

1. During the course of spring football (college) practice, the coaches show an obvious concern for the players lack of willingness to take punishment and handle the unexpected. Hand to hand combat specialists with pugli clubs roam the practice, unsuspectedly attacking players in drill or scrimmage. Although nothing of a severe nature occurred, the all conference quarterback was lost for the remaining week because of a concussion. He was blindsided with a pugli stick during pass scrimmage. He was also lost to the baseball team for the remainder of their schedule (a month and a half).
   - Did the coach deviate from the rules of the game by creating his own format to teach certain traits?
   - Was the teaching format reasonable for the level of participation and age of the competitors?
   - Was the standard of care appropriate to the activity?

2. Tennis is always a popular elective in the physical education program. Despite being limited to only two courts, the thirty students have been taught fundamentals by spacing 15 players on either side of the net. Stroke, service and toss hit drills are a little crowded but at least everyone is kept busy. The last stroking did result in a few elbows being hit after the follow through, and one student got hit in the eye with a ball.
   - Did the instructor fail to exercise care for the safety of the students?
   - Was there deviation from the rules of the game?
   - Does the teaching format suggest an unreasonable learning atmosphere?

3. As part of the rainy day activity for the elementary class, the teacher has planned a leap frog relay. She explains the rules of the race and selects two students for demonstration. During the demonstration, she stresses to all students the necessity for keeping their arms straight during the support phase and while the vault is in progress. However, when the relay commences, a student flexes his arms and the vaulter falls to the mat breaking an arm. The parents are irate.
   - Did the teacher provide adequate instruction and supervision?
   - Did the student incur any inherent risk in the activity?
   - Is there an obvious risk in leap-frog?
   - Is it possible for a coach or teacher to foresee and forewarn about the risks or hazards in an activity?

4. The winter has been tiresome and diversion seems appropriate. The class will be divided in half and play en mass. Essentially, the game will be a combination of bombardment, dodgeball and basketball. A volleyball will be more appropriate than a basketball because it is easier to grip and throw with one hand. A few participants suffer a bloody nose due to errant throws, but as evidenced by the shouting, a good time is had by all.
   • Can the modification of activity with familiar activities create an unsafe, unreasonable play environment?

5. Two practice fields are separated by a deep trench. A whistle signalled the lineman to a scrimmage on the west field. As they charged up the slope to the play field, they were blinded by the glare of the sun. Suddenly, on the command of the coach, the blinded players were cut down by a variety of blocks and blockers. Needless to say, there were some injuries.
   • Does the devising of such format and associated risks constitute a natural and obvious aspect of the sport?

Risk Management Suggestions

• Make an effort to retain a voluntary aspect to activity participation.
• Develop practice plans, orientation format, explanations and demonstrations to the age, maturation and comprehension level of the participants. The aim should be on assuring that the participant knows and perceives the risks and hazards inherent to the activity.
• Safety rules, standards and practices should be developed and supervised to minimize risk and enhance performance.
• The games rules and conduct proscribed by those rules should be thoroughly understood by the instructor and communicated by work and deed to the student.
• The use of charts and/or posters (such as the NCAA football rules poster) can be an effective technique to help minimize risks associated with protective equipment. Similar charts could be developed for a wide variety of sports: Hockey, Baseball, Wrestling, Gymnastics, Tennis, Field Hockey, and others.
• Reckless behavior should not be condoned; whereas, sportsmanship and fair play should be positively reinforced.
• The activity specialist should be familiar with the natural and obvious risks which might be incurred in the activity, foreseeing and forewarning against such risks.

- Modifying techniques and developing new and different teaching formats should be done within the rules of the game, considering time segments, number of players, equipment, infractions, etc.
- Supervision may necessitate active intervention to prevent injury.
- Attempts should be made to identify, monitor and control participants whose personal characteristics reflect violence or the inclination toward violent sport acts.

Selected References

Gowen, Thomas L., "Sports Programs and Injuries: Liability Since Rutter," *Pennsylvania Law Journal-Reporter*, April 5, 1982, Vol. V. No. 13, pp. 2 and 10.

Nabozny v. Barnhill, 334 N.E. 2d 258.

Tucker, Neil R., "Assumption of Risk and Vicarious Liability in Personal Injury Actions brought by Professional Athletes," *Duke Law Journal, Vol. 1980, No. 4, pp. 742-766.*

Law and Amateur Sports: Issues of the 80's, Hyatt Regency, Indianapolis, August 1981, pp. 53-62.

CHAPTER VIII
Supervision

If the most common phenomena precipitating a litigation of liability against school personnel is PUPIL INJURY, then the question of supervision is the most common related casual factor. A report at the 1970 AAHPER Convention in New Orleans stated that supervision is usually raised in every liability case. And, it further stressed that the question is usually a matter of quality and quantity.

Simplistically, the term supervision means DIRECTION, INSPECTION, and CRITICAL EVALUATION, according to Webster's *Third New International Dictionary*. The term has expanded greatly since its appearance in education in the early seventies of the last century. James Humphrey says, "the term supervision is directly related to the teacher-pupil learning situation." (Humphrey: 4) Carter Good, *Dictionary of Education*, defines supervision: all efforts of designated school officials toward providing leadership to teachers and other educational workers in the improvement of instruction; involves stimulation of professional growth and development of teachers, the selection and revision of educational objectives, materials of instruction, methods of teaching and evaluation of instruction.

Regardless of the definition, there exist a few common threads: 1) supervision is related to the teacher/pupil learning situations; 2) wherein, the leadership is provided to the appropriate individual(s) to effectively direct, inspect and evaluate their activity (3) to a level of improvement.

It is regularly maintained that schools have a duty to supervise the conduct of students on premises at all times and to enforce relevant rules and regulations. (Enos: 1-15)

Luce v. Board of Education. A young girl with a history of previous injuries was injured during a jump-the-stick relay in a physical education class. The teacher and principal had been informed by the parents that the girl should not participate in courses or activities where she might fall. The teacher was found negligent because the teacher was to "exercise reasonable care to prevent injuries and to assign pupils to activities within their abilities and properly and adequately supervise the activities." (2 A.D. 2d 1975)

Again, in *Keesee v. Board of Education*, the teacher in physical education was found negligent. Guidelines within the course syllabus, regarding the number of participant, were not followed and injury resulted. Although the intent was to get more girls to play, the additional number created a poor situation for the novice performer. (235 NYS 2d 306).

A school employee, on leave of absence for major surgery, was subsequently injured. She was returning across the gym floor when she was bumped and knocked to the floor by student(s). The supervising teacher was not present. The court found the district negligent in conducting an activity without adequate supervision and without maintaining proper control. (633 P 2d 1287).

A test for determining negligence in supervision centers on whether a reasonably prudent person in the place of teacher could have reason to believe that injury might occur. (Harty: 320).

Supervision cases alleging negligence may be categorized as those 1) failing to make and enforce rules, 2) those failing to provide competent supervision and 3) post-injury handling. (Harty: 321). James Harty goes on to elaborate on each of the points:

a. Make and enforce rules: for student safety; failure to make rules can result in liability; failing to enforce rules; principal may have a duty to initiate rules if the board fails to act; teachers have a duty to follow the rules for the safety of the student. (Harty: 321-322).

b. Competent supervision: personnel adequately trained to assume duties assigned; sufficient number to cover needs of situation; competent officials; wary of assigning physical education duties to personnel not certified in the area; coaches should not be assigned to a sport unless they have experience in that sport sufficient to protect participants from unreasonable risk. (Harty; 322-323).

When competent supervision is provided, questions may arise as to the quality of that supervision: was the supervisor absent; was the injury foreseeable; would the supervisor's presence have prevented the injury; was there a failure to supervise in a proper manner. (Harty: 323-324)

c. Post-injury treatment: secure or provide reasonable medical care as soon as possible under the circumstances; don't assume the role of the physician; don't force improper medical care in a non-emergency situation; having students participate contrary to physician's note; deciding that medical assistance is not needed. (Harty: 324-325).

The legal aspect of supervision can be explained as follows: "Courts have generally held schools or their agents liable for injuries received during the course of regular school events which resulted from the school's or its agents' failure to provide a reasonably safe environment, failure to warn participants of known hazards or to remove known danger where possible, failure to properly instruct participants in the activity, or failure to provide supervision adequate for the type of activity and the ages of the participants involved."

"This does not, however, place schools and teachers under a burden to provide constant supervision nor does it mandate supervision of children involved in activities of their own making off the school grounds." (DEASL: 10).

Having reviewed some of the components and circumstances relative to supervision, the problem in this area is evident. Cases can be found where the supervisor was absent and the lack of supervision was easily established. However, when an instructor is present, then the quality and nature of supervision may be under examination, as in Beck v. San Francisco Unified District. (37 Cal Rptr. 471) A student was injured when struck by two fellow students while attending the annual school carnival. In the circumstance 23 teachers had been assigned to the carnival and 5 or 6 were in the area of the attack just before the student was struck. Testimony was that there had been no trouble at previous carnivals. Within the contrasting examples the problem is reflected: "The problem is when supervision provided is adequate numerically, but is not under the circumstances competent and experienced enough to handle responsibilities assigned." (Liebee: 75) The matter is a question of quantity and quality. It must be reasonable in both degree and quality.

At least a first step in providing good supervision is the hiring of qualified personnel. And, the qualifications should be commensurate to the activity and attendant risks. This is easy to say but is actually more complex. For instance, the most obvious of the qualified in the school setting is the professional who has completed the standards for degree and certification. Then we may have paraprofessionals on the scene providing services and certain tasks. Or, standards for certifying coaches may exist in a variety of formats. The standards may be different for head coaches and assistants and be in the form of an authorization. As an example, the State of Iowa has a Coaching Authorization:

Applicants for the coaching authorization shall have completed the following requirements:

1. . . . one semester credit hour or 10 contact hours in a course relating to knowledge and understanding of the structure and function of the human body in relation to physical activity.
2. . . . one semester credit hour or 10 contact hours . . . to knowledge or understanding of human growth and development of children and growth in relation to physical activity.
3. . . . two semester credit hours or 20 contact hours . . . prevention care of athletic injuries and medical and safety problems . . . in addition to physical activity.
4. . . . one semester credit hour or 10 contact hours relating to . . . techniques and theory of coaching interscholastic athletics. (State of Iowa, Department of Public Instruction).

Having met the requirements and paid the fee, the applicant receives a card which emphasizes certain stipulations, such as not being authorized to be a varsity head coach in certain sports; whereas, it is valid for assisting in any sport.

The qualifications of coaches and what coaches should have done on a little league baseball team has prompted some legislative consideration for volunteer coaches. A recent suit against a volunteer little league coach has caused a problem in staffing "Little Clubs" in some New Jersey communities. A bill to limit recovery and protect the volunteer coach has been proposed. It provides that no volunteer athletic coach, manager, or sports team official be held liable in "any civil action" as a result of their responsibilities as a coach or manager. (Blodgett, Nancy, "Good Samaritan", *Law Scope*, 1986). They must first have participated in a "safety orientation and training program" established by the league or team with which they are affilliated, and there is an exception that they still can be found liable for gross negligence. (Blodgett, N. *Law Scope*, 1986)

Several valuable points can be taken from the Iowa Coaching Authorization Plan and the New Jersey volunteer coach legislation. First, individuals with specific qualifications are told what they can and cannot do. Secondly, safety orientation and training programs are essential to the standard of performance for the volunteer coach.

Howard Liebee made some observations about supervision in "Tort Liability for Injuries to Pupils," (1965). These observations still warrant consideration: "Responsibility of every school authority to guard against (injury) occurrence to the full extent of his ability. Adequacy of supervision depends on the circumstances of each case, governed by reasonableness. Consequently, mere formulation and posting of rules and regulations regarding equipment and facilities may not be enough to satisfy supervision requirements." (Liebee: 75) Some comparable factors were addressed by Hudgins and Mallois: "Employ responsible people; know the extent of one's authority; be sensitive to potential problems; exercise reasonable supervision . . . Risks attendant to the specific activity; precautions necessary for safety of participant; particular supervisory requirement for grade level involved."

These points imply at least two basic qualitative factors. That is, a school can take a first step to providing adequate supervision by hiring certified (qualified) personnel. Also, if a particular accident could have been avoided by more adequate supervision and if it could have been provided, then responsibility of the school has not been provided. (Liebee: 75) The quality of supervision can be further enhanced by careful examination of what is expected of the instructor or coach. In addition to the attendant risks, safety precautions and supervisory requirement mentioned previously, he/she is expected to consider:

a. necessary skills.
b. level of maturity expected.
c. as an activity increases in risk the foreseeability of danger imposes an added standard of care.
d. hazard or danger should be anticipated (Mallois: 61)

In some instances modification or flexibility in the instructor's approach is essential. The skill component in an activity may range from being immaterial or determinative. Contrast tennis and gymnastics: it's evident that participant skill, spotting and performance environment impose a degree of supervision and precaution to gymnastics beyond that essential to tennis. Another sport imposing stricter supervisory standards because of risk and participant skill is swimming. *Exceeding the skill of the young athlete* in gymnastics may in itself be the *proximate cause*. Landers v. School District, 383 NE 645. Contributory negligence will provide small comfort . . . if the injured is very young. Generally, the court will not view seriously . . .unless the child is in early teens. (Gowen: 10)

Should the teacher-coach be interested in some solid safety suggestions, Hudgins and Vacca provide the following.

1. Employ responsible people.
2. Know the extent of one's authority.
3. Be familiar with rights of one's subordinates.
4. Award contracts to competent firms doing business with the school.
5. Be sensitive to potential problems.
6. Gear work to the students.
7. Teach attitudes and responsibilities.
8. Make periodic inspections.
9. Report problems promptly.
10. Avoid overcrowding.
11. Get rid of junk.
12. Exercise reasonable supervision.

Summary

- Pupil injury is the most common event precipitating a litigation against schools and teachers and the nature of supervision is usually raised in all the cases.
- Supervision is direction, inspection and critical evaluation.
- Supervision is related to the teacher/pupil learning situation; 2) wherein, the leadership is provided to the appropriate individual(s) to effectively direct, inspect and evaluate their activity to a level of improvement.
- Schools must exercise reasonable care to prevent injuries.
- Schools must assign pupils to activities within their abilities.
- The teacher-coach should always be present, and should not leave an area unsupervised.
- Make and enforce rules for student safety, the teacher should make certain that the rules are carried out.
- Competent supervision includes qualified personnel, appropriate student to teacher ratio, proper technique, teacher presence and foreseeability.
- The supervisory dilemma is when there appears to be an adequate number of supervisors but the quality of the action (supervision) is in question.
- A first step in providing good supervision is hiring qualified personnel suitable for the circumstance.
- Certified teacher-coaches, authorizations and volunteer coaches reflect the variety in qualified personnel.

- Some qualified personnel may be restricted as to what their role may be, and they should be instructed as to what they should or should not do.
- Some components of good supervision are knowing:
  Risks specific to the activity.
  Precautions necessary for safety.
  Supervisory requirement for each grade level.
  Necessary skills per activity.
  Level of maturity expected.
  Risk, foreseeability and standard of care increases as the activity increases in risk.
  Hazards or dangers should be anticipated.

- Skill of the participant may be a determining factor in gymnastics, swimming and other high risk activities and impose a higher standard of care in supervision.
- Generally, the court will not view contributory negligence as serious if the injured child is very young.
- Along with other safety guidelines the educator-coach should know the extent of one's authority, be familiar with the rights of subordinates, contract competent firms for business with the school, and teach attitudes and responsibilities.

You're in Their Shoes

1. The heavy overcast and persistent misting has forced activity indoors. Time is a factor if the class is to have any activity. Badminton equipment is readily available and if nets are not utilized fun can be had by hitting the rubber tipped outdoor shuttlecock back and forth. Poor lighting and overcrowding wasn't a deterrent to fun. However, a serious eye injury did occur.
   - Was the injury inherent to the activity?
   - Is it good supervisory judgement to conduct the activity in the performance setting?
   - Was proper consideration given to selection of equipment and modification of activity to the safety of the performer.

2. As a volunteer coach for "Little League," the experience has been extremely rewarding and gratifying. However, a particularly critical situation developed when a 13 year old boy was hit in the eye with a ball. The boy had been shifted from second base to the outfield, before the accident. It was maintained that the boy should have been given flip-down sunglasses or in-

structed on how to use his glove to shield the sun from his eyes before being moved from the infield. It's enough to discourage coaches from trying to teach young players who are not outstanding athletes.

- Is the standard of care for volunteer coaches different than coaches hired for the task?
- Is the standard of care of volunteer coaches comparable to the ordinary citizen lending assistance to others?
- What duty exists relative to safety and training programs?

3. Prom night was again a success with over 250 students in attendance. The band played a variety of music which afforded an opportunity for all to dance and enjoy. It was especially gratifying to have 25 teachers in attendance although the largest percentage seemed to congregate around the refreshment table. When a fight broke out at the far end of the gym, it was tough to find any faculty. If students hadn't stepped in, the consequences would have been more serious than the loss of a few teeth and a broken nose.

- Does a teacher to pupils ratio exist which is representative of good supervision?
- Can good supervisory technique be independent of numerical relationships?
- Or, do circumstances impact on the degree and quality of supervision.
- Is there a duty to preplan supervisory procedure to address numerical ratios, crowd control, flow patterns, emergencies and other contingencies?

Risk Management Suggestions

- Preplanning should include the identification of common interactions which typically result in supervisory problems or conflict:
    Pupil conduct
    Accident/emergency care
    Competitive activities
    Dangerous and hazardous learning situations (apparatus, aquatics, combatives, to mention a few)
    General learning experiences (field trips, etc.)
    Facilities/ equipment

- Having recognized potential conflict situations, a few basic considerations could initiate planning for supervision. Some suggestions or opinions, not intended to be all inclusive:

What is the nature of *the activity* - passive, active, low stress, high stress, movement and force patterns, risks, hazards.

What is the nature of the *the facility* - Space, safety engineering standards, environment (aquatic, ice, bluffs, rock ledges, etc.), risks, hazards, vastness or restrictiveness.

What is the nature of *the equipment* - safety performance standards, size to user, skill level, quality status (newness), functional status technical requirements, risks, hazards.

What is the nature of *the participant* - competency level, health status, infirmities, personality, characteristics, (aggressive, violent, passive, immature, mature) leadership traits or lack there of, social and group traits (antagonistic attitudes, gangs or clubs which may be problematic), special traits or characteristics.

What is the nature of *the methodology* homogeneous grouping by age, skill, size, etc., subgrouping, rotations, group leaders, paraprofessional progressive, lead-up, command, emergency procedures.

- A supervisor should always be present.
- A supervisor should not leave an area unsupervised.
- Dangerous equipment, facilities, or playground equipment should not be used without supervision.
- Swimming pools, gymnasium and other (attractive) dangerous areas should be locked and resecured when not in use and supervised.
- Dangerous equipment or instruments should be locked or secured when not in use and supervised.
- Attempt to clarify the extent of personnel authority and assigned duty, especially when sharing facilities with other teachers, programs and/or agencies.
- Develop and post guidelines and policies which would help support supervision efforts and not tend to replace them.
- Develop charts for all activities depicting what consistutes proper equipment. The NCAA chart on football equipment is an example of a good risk management technique (non-directive). (Supplied through the courtesy of the NCAA.)
- Consider the development of authorization standards for critical tasks within a program. It could be parallel to the Iowa plan, developed by staff consensus and involve gymnastics, swimming, weight lifting, volunteer support personnel or other critical instructional areas.
- Develop a technique for periodic inspection, keeping in mind

67

that *the nature* of component of supervision may influence the frequency of the inspection.

- Staff should be indoctrinated with the concept that as an activity increases in risk the standard of care may also increase. This not only occurs between sport activities; for instance, badminton to football, but also within an activity (passive to intense competition).
- Safe-guards should be exercised when returning a student to activity following an illness or injury. Records should indicate not only when they returned but how they were phased in to the activity. This may alleviate a possible accusation of aggrevating the condition or return to full performance too soon.
- Attitudes and responsibility should be taught to students and staff. They are not just teacher or just coaches. They are Sportucators, Physical Activity Scientists, who through the educative process help to affect behavior.

If they do it wrong, there is alot of - - ACHE
If they do it right, they can TEACH
COACH and
REACH the child

Supervision should be a reasonable, responsible educative circumstance.

Selected References

Beck v. San Francisco Unified District, 37 Cal. Rptr. 471 Blodgett, N., "Good Samaritan Bill Shields Unpaid Coaches," *Law Scope*, 1986.

—————, *1985 Deskback Encyclopedia of American School Law*, Data Research Inc. Rosemount, Minn., 1985, pp.2-4.

Enos, D.F., *Supervision: Who's Responsible or the Law and the Irresponsible Somebody*, U.S. Dept. HEW, March, 1975, pp. 1-15.

Gowen, Thomas, "Sports Programs and Injuries: Liability Since Rutter," *Pennsylvannia Law Journal Reporter* April 5, 1982. Vol. V. No. 13, pp. 2 and 10.

Harty, James, "School Liability for Athletic Injuries: Duty, Causation and Defense," *Washburn Law Journal*. Vol 21, 1982, pp. 315-341.

Hudgins, M.C., and Vacca, R. *Laws and Education* Michie Co., Charlotteville, VA, 1979, p. 93.

Humphrey, James, *Principles and Techniques of Supervision in Physical Education*, W.C. Brown Co. Dubuque, Ia. 1972, p.4.

Keese v. Board of Education, 235 NYS 2d 306.

Landers v. School District, 383 N.E. 2d 645.

Liebee, H. *Tort Liability for Injuries to Pupils*, Campus Publishers, Ann Arbor, Michigan, 1965, p.75.

Luci v. Board of Education, 2 A.D. 1975, 159 NYS 2d 965

Mallois, H.C. "The Physical Education and the Law,"*The Physical Educator*, May 1975, Vol. 32, p. 61.

Charts courtesy of:

Halter, M., Coaching Authorization, Department of Public Instruction, State of Iowa, Des Moines, Iowa.

_____, 1985 Football Rules, National Collegiate Athletic Association, Mission, Kansas.

_____, 1986 Football Equipment Standards, Naitonal Collegiate Athletic Association, Mission, Kansas.

STATE OF IOWA • DEPARTMENT OF PUBLIC INSTRUCTION

GRIMES STATE OFFICE BUILDING • DES MOINES. IOWA 50319-0146

IOWA
a place to grow

ROBERT D. BENTON, Ed.D., STATE SUPERINTENDENT
David H. Bechtel, M. S., Administrative Assistant
JAMES E. MITCHELL, Ph.D., DEPUTY SUPERINTENDENT

DATE: April 15, 1985

TO: Applicants for the coaching authorization

FROM: Teacher Education and Certification Division

SUBJECT: Coaching Authorization

Applicants for the coaching authorization shall have completed the following requirements:

1) Successful completion of one semester credit hour or 10 contact hours in a course relating to knowledge and understanding of the structure and function of the human body in relation to physical activity.

2) Successful completion of one semester credit hour or 10 contact hours in a course relating to knowledge and understanding of human growth and development of children and youth in relation to physical activity.

3) Successful completion of two semester credit hours or 20 contact hours in a course relating to knowledge and understanding of the prevention and care of athletic injuries and medical and safety problems relating to physical activity.

4) Successful completion of one semester credit hour or 10 contact hours relating to knowledge and understanding of the techniques and theory of coaching interscholastic athletics.

Any person interested in the coaching authorization shall submit records of credit to the Department of Public Instruction for an evaluation in terms of the required courses or contact hours.

The coaching authorization shall be valid for five years, and it shall expire five years from the date of issuance. The fee for the coaching authorization shall be $15.

Enclosed please find the application form to apply for the coaching authorization.

Sincerely,

Merrill Halter

Merrill Halter, Consultant
Teacher Education and Certification

MH/ab
Enclosure: Application

State of Iowa
DEPARTMENT OF PUBLIC INSTRUCTION
Teacher Education and Certification Division
Grimes State Office Building
Des Moines, Iowa 50319

APPLICATION FOR COACHING AUTHORIZATION

Name:_____ _____ _____ _____

        Last   First   Middle   Maiden

Address: _____ _____ _____ _____

        Number and Street   City   State   Zip Code

                         Business or
Home Phone: School Phone: Social Security Number:

___/_____   ___/_____   _____ - _____ - _____

NOTE:
1. A fee of $15.00 is required. DO NOT SEND CASH. Send check or money order
    made payable to the Commissioner of Public Instruction.
2. Attach transcripts or verification you have completed the four-course
    requirements for the coaching authorization.

_____ _____ 19____

Signature of Applicant   Date Signed

Return application to: Teacher Education and Certification Division
                      Department of Public Instruction
                      Grimes State Office Building
                      Des Moines, Iowa 50319

CHAPTER IX
Release of Liability and Informed Consent

Waivers

With the frequency of liability litigation and the large sums of money awarded, it is little wonder that concerned professionals seek relief from liability. They look beyond their own expertise and common sense for methods or techniques which would afford additional protection against the chance of litigation. Also, because of the substantial risk to participants, the teacher, coach, or event organizer often considers *release of liability* as the method of protection they seek. The method they hope will absolve them from any injury or loss. And, more often than not there may be some confusion or misunderstanding about the effectiveness of the technique, especially with the waiver and release of liability.

It is generally recognized and accepted that such waiver and release forms are viewed as contracts and as such are not binding where minors are concerned. Opinion in the Doyle v. Bowdoin College, 403 A 2d 1206, case stated, "This court has held that a parent, or guardian, cannot release the child's or ward's, cause of action." Yet, in many instances, the technique is endorsed by some lawyers, encouraged by some school administrators and used with some enthusiasm by the teacher-coach. The enthusiasm may reflect the attitude, "It is better than nothing."

An obvious question is, why use the "contract from immunity" technique? A possible answer may be that it reflects a level of reason or effort to inform the parent(s) and receive their response in form of the signature. Or, it may be good administrative policy to use such a technique in contrast to not using any such process. It may indeed be better than nothing. Such a process may also demonstrate concern on the part of school and personnel for the welfare of the student. Tom Ross, *Law & Sports Conference*, 1984 elaborates on the reasons for using such a waiver: "It is a good administrative procedure because it provides useful information . . . that parents had granted permission . . . warning of the possibility of an injury and the risk factor has been explained . . . that the institution is not an insurer of safety . . . that the school is not responsible for medical and related bills . . . can be used

71

to distinguish between mere happening of an accident and negligent injuries . . . and may actually bind the parent(s) to preclude parents from instituting a lawsuit."

Dekalb v. White (260 SE 2d 853) offers some supportive opinion. Although the Dekalb County Superior Court discounted the father's signed waiver, the Supreme Court (Georgia) held written waiver of eligibility to be a reflection of the policy of the school system for consideration of all students.

Three important items to note are that (1) the waiver reflected the policy of the school system, (2) the father was treated according to school policy, and (3) the father was informed of and understood the terms. (Dekalb v. White: 854)

It is apparent that some justification for using waiver of release from liability does exist. Regardless, there is still some confusion from the standpoint of the sporarcator (teacher-coach). This confusion results from not fully understanding what the waiver actually is and why it may not be effective in some matters. There are some distinguishing factors which will help in understanding the *waiver*:

1. It is a contract or consensual agreement. (Contracts providing for immunity from negligence must be construed strictly since they are not favorities of the law, 403 A2d 1206).
2. As a contract, the language and structure should be of strict construct. (. . . must spell out intention of parties with greatest of particularity and show intent to release from liability beyond doubt by expressed stipulation, and no inference from general inpart can establish such release, 403 A2d 1206).
3. Only those who are competent and can manage their own affairs may enter into the agreement. (. . . parent or guardian cannot release child's or ward's cause of action, 403 A2d 1206).
4. Responsibility for injury resulting from negligent act(s) can still be present. (A state may sometimes disregard wishes of parents "When [a child's] physical . . . health is jeopardized." . . . instances are rare . . . premised on child abuse and neglect . . . rather than upon a mere difference of rational opinion, 490 F. Supp. 948 (1980).
5. Exculpatory language exists, which is asking someone to be relieved of responsibility. (Weistart: 965).
6. Waivers have been successful in sports business, special events and professional sports. (When exculpatory clauses have been signed by participants in athletic activities, they have, as a general rule, been upheld with the courts consid-

ering and applying . . . the same principles noted . . . Weistart: 966).

At first glance, it would appear that a waiver is an effective mechanism for abrogating responsibility, while maximizing the participation of the individual and program. However, responsibility is not lost, it merely assumes a different posture. Such waivers and exculpatory contracts cannot insulate a person from liability resulting from wilful, wanton or reckless misconduct. (Weistart: 966).

And, the Poole v. South Plainfield Board of Education addresses, in part, the question of responsibility beyond a release or waiver. A student, born with one kidney, sought damages when he was denied the right to participate in high school interscholastic wrestling. Both Richard and his parents wanted him to participate, even after they were made aware of the school system's concern over possible kidney injury. Despite protests and an offer to sign a waiver by the student and parents, the Board decided to deny participation.

R. J. Cirafesi (Board's attorney) expressed responsibility beyond such waivers in his comment, "Although, at first blush, a complete release and waiver would appear to resolve the problem at hand, such an approach side-steps the basic question of responsibility. In other words, in my opinion, the Board of Education cannot abrogate its responsibility towards the pupils in question by placing the entire burden of responsibility upon the pupils and parents." (490 F. Supp. 948).

Recognizing that it is the opinion of the defense attorney, the judgement of the court also recognizes the responsibility beyond the release by stating, "The Board's responsibility is to see that he does not pursue this course in a foolish manner. They therefore have a duty to alert Richard and his parents to the dangers involved and require them to deal with the matter rationally. . . . Whatever duty the Board may have had . . . was satisfied once it became clear that the Pooles knew of the dangers involved and rationally reached a decision to encourage their son's participation in interscholastic wrestling." (490 F. Supp. 948).

In essence, the responsibility or duty beyond the waiver was met when the pupil and parents *knew the dangers* and *rationally made their decision.*

Weistart has identified the necessary components of a waiver in order for it to be enforceable:

a. Waiving party must know the terms of the release.

b. Waiver (language) must be conspicuous.

c. It (waiver) must result from free and open bargaining.

d. And, its express terms must be applicable to the particular misconduct of the party whose potential liability is waived,

e. It cannot protect the party from liability for damages resulting from wanton, intentional or reckless misconduct.

f. The contract (waiver) may be repudiated if the signee is a minor. (Weistart: 966).

Specialist in the physical activity sciences, namely teachers and coaches, would do well to consider the principles emphasized in waiver related cases. This, the waiver, may appear to be a way out, a relief from litigation, but it has its pitfalls. They appear to be enforceable, but their structure and use is complex, especially where there is strong public policy or where the party obtaining the agreement is in a clear dominant position to the person signing away his rights. (Weistart: 966).

Some guidelines for the physical educator and coach (sportucators) are:

1. The decision to use a "waiver and release" from liability should not be capricious.

2. Engage legal counsel to determine its necessity and language structure. It should not be designed and/or drafted by the school, unless the personnel are specifically qualified to do so.

3. The person waiving must be fully informed.

4. The clause or statement of release must be clearly visible, up-front, not hidden in small print somewhere in the document.

5. The individual should have free, open bargaining to sign the waiver. It is to be voluntary with no compulsion on the part of the actor to sign.

6. The statement should be directly related to the misconduct (or conduct) of the party involved.

7. Only a person who can legally handle their own affairs (lawfully competent) may sign. The contract, if the signer is a minor, may be repudiated.

8. A waiver cannot protect a party from liability resulting from willful, wanton, intentional or reckless misconduct.

Although the waiver and release of liability appears to be more applicable to sports businesses, it is not without significance in education and the physical activity sciences of physical education and sport. Basically, the law tries to protect the minor and minors are viewed as incapable of entering contracts, except in certain defined areas. However, the waiver, when dealing with parent and minor, could be viewed as a good administrative procedure. It would be a reasonable measure to inform or give notice to the parent and student of potential risks of injury. It at least shows that permission for participation had been granted by the parent(s). It may also inform the parties about the availability of medical treatment and/or compensation, and who is responsible for those aspects. The waiver may help in distinguishing between a mere happening or occurrence of an accident and negligent injuries of a willful wanton nature.

Bear in mind the waiver's construct is strict, constitutes a contract, and should be developed and used only through legal consul. One may want to consider "informed consent" as a desirable alternative because a good parallel exists between the "waiver and informed consent."

Informed Consent

Informed consent, as a technique, has been basically associated with research and human subjects in research, and is a fundamental part of Health Education and Welfare research guidelines. As with its counterpart the waiver, informed consent is also an agreement, usually an agreement to participate in some research, procedure or experimentation. However, the characteristics and advantages of informed consent make it a viable alternative to the waiver.

What is "informed consent" is best defined by the Code of Federal Regulations (CFR):

"Informed Consent means that knowing consent of an individual or his legal authorized representative, so situated as to be able to exercise free power of choice without undue inducement or any element of force, fraud, deceit or other forms of constraint or coercion." (45 CFR 46.103C)

Significant in the consent of an individual to participate is their *knowing* consent. The individual must actually understand, perceive and be aware of the many aspects of the total experience they're about to be involved with. The question of *knowing* could be for the court to resolve. It should also be recognized that it is the *individual or legal, authorized representative* who may exercise the consent. This facet should have instant appeal for the educator, physical educator and/or coach.

Elementary School, informed consent needs parent consent and signature along with child assent.

Junior High School, informed consent needs parent signature and child assent and signature.

High School, informed consent needs, parent signature and child signature.

College and University, informed consent needs only, student signature.

The Code of Federal Regulations explains in more detail the essential components of "informed consent."

"Except as provided elsewhere in this or other subparts, *no investigator may involve* a human being *as a subject in research covered by these regulations unless* the investigator has *obtained informed consent of the subject* or the subject's legal authorized representative. An investigator shall seek consent only under circumstances that provide the prospective subject or the representative sufficient *opportunity to consider* whether or not to participate and that *minimize the possibility of coercion or undue influence.* The information that is given to the subject or representative shall be in *language understandable* to the subject or the representative. *No informed consent,* whether oral or written, *may include any exculpatory language* through which the subject or the representative is made to waiver or appear to waive or appear to waive any of the subject's legal rights, or releases or appears to release the investigator, the sponsor, the institution or its agents from liability or negligence." (45 CFR 46: 103C)

This paragraph sets forth the circumstances which must be met in obtaining informed consent. When met, these circumstances verify that consent has been exercised. Teachers, coaches and investigators in research must be aware of these facets of consent:

- provide opportunity to consider whether or not to participate.
- minimize coercion or undue influence as to whether to participate, or not to participate.
- provide understandable language or information to the subject or its representative.
- not include *exculpatory language, oral or written, in the consent. (*to clear from alleged fault or guilt . . . absolve, exonerate, acquit. *Websters Dictionary*).

At this point it is important to note that the individual or its authorized representative is entering into agreement and neither is being asked to give up, release or waive any legal right or responsibility. Basically, their willingness to participate is being sought after having been informed about the research or activity they are sought for. And, depending upon the educational level, the parent and/or student are giving consent to participate, according to information provided by these basic elements. An oral, or written 'informed consent' must have these basic elements: (45 CFR 46, 103C)

1. A fair explanation of the procedures to be followed and their purposes.
2. A description of any attendant discomforts and risks reasonably to be expected.
3. A description of any benefits reasonably to be expected.
4. A disclosure of any appropriate alternative procedures that might be advantageous for the subject.
5. An offer to answer any inquiries concerning the procedures, (confidentiality of records, extent, maintained);
6. An instruction that the person is free to withdraw his consent and to discontinue participation in the project or activity at any time without prejudice to the subject.
7. With respect to biomedical or behavioral research which may result in physical injury, an explanation as to whether compensation and medical treatment is available if physical injury occurs and, if so, what it consists of or where further information may be obtained.

If neither medical treatment nor compensation are available as a normal procedure, general wording may inform the participants: "I understand that in the event of physical injury resulting from the research procedure, financial compensation is not available and medical treatment is not provided free of charge."

In addition, the agreement (informed consent), written or oral, entered into by the participant should not include exculpatory language through which the participant is made to waive, or appear to waive, any of his legal rights, including any release of the institution, or its agents from liability for negligence (45 CFR 46.103C).

The utilization of this technique in research programs, fitness testing, exercise prescription and similar programs is essential and important because human subjects are involved. However, there is evidence in the literature, commercial undertakings and from convention programs, that there is increased interest in "informed consent." It is being used to inform parents and students

77

of the attendant benefits and risks in sports, especially in football. Considering the acceptability of signatures (legal representative and for the child), nature of information (procedures, risks, benefits) to communicate and the fact that the involved is not waiving a legal right, it is easy to see why 'informed consent' is being applied to the sport activity scene with growing popularity. In fact, there are formats commercially available in the form of films and representative letters to assist in developing an 'informed consent' approach.

Summary

- "Waiver and release of liability" is considered a contract with strict language and construct.
- The parent or guardian cannot sign away the right of the minor.
- The use of the "waiver" is sometimes encouraged as a good administrative technique, to inform the parent, to have a signature response, and to demonstrate a level of reasonable concern.
- "Waiver of Liability" may be an effective instrument when competent adults freely enter into the agreement and willingly waive their rights.
- Willingness to inform, distinguishing between type of behavior, providing an understanding of terms and conditions, and reflecting school policy, these may be extended functions of "waiver."
- Agreements, waivers and informed consent, must be free of coercion and result from free and open bargaining.
- Although a signed waiver may be executed, "responsibility beyond" the waiver may still exist, such responsibility may be to protect the participant from some foolish course of action.
- A critical aspect of both the "waiver" and "informed consent" is whether the parties actually "understand" or "know" the terms of the agreement.
- The decision to incorporate a "waiver" should not be capricious. Consultation with an attorney can provide counsel about guidelines, critical areas, language, and construction.
- Informed consent offers the advantage of acceptable (legally) signatures by parent and/or child.
- Informed consent is void of 'exculpatory language.' The participant is not being asked to waive a legal right.
- 'Informed Consent' is the "knowing consent" of an individual on legal representative to participate.

- *"Knowing consent"* may also include the information and knowledge that compensation, medical treatment, or/and insurance is not available despite the attendant procedures, benefits and risks as presented.
- Legal counsel should be engaged to insure that the parameters and intent of informed consent are met.

You're In Their Shoes

1. A suit is brought by a parent against a school system so that his son could play football in his senior year in high school. The parent signed a waiver which limited the number of years of eligibility son had in his high school career:

   ". . . I further relieve the high school, its officials and teachers, of any responsibility of this decision I have made to hold him in eighth grade . . ."

   The written waiver reflected the policy of the school system to consider all students that pass the eighth grade as ninth graders, despite the fact that the eighth grade courses are repeated.
   • Was an attempt made to distinguish the type of behavior which classified all students in a like manner?
   • Was the parent treated according to the school system policy?
   • Was the parent informed of and understood the terms under which the student would be allowed to repeat the eight grade courses?

2. Waiver and Release

COUNTRY FEDERAL LOAN
10,000 METER RUN

DATE: Saturday, June 16, 1986   TIME: 8:00 a.m.

PLACE: Dountown Sport City, Illinois, during Harvets Fest

COURSE: Leave downtown Sport City on city streets to Brewers Park
    ...continue through Brewers Park to Elm Tree Park
    ...return to starting point. There will be 4 water stations
throughout the course. Time splits will be given at 1, 2,
3, and 4 miles.

ENTRY FEE: $5.00 before June 15—$6.00 on day of race
    $2.00 for members of Road Runner Club.

NO REFUNDS

PRE-REGISTRATION: Mail entry form as indicated below. We appreciate and encourage pre-registration. Those who do so may pick up their race packets between 6:00 and 7:00 a.m. race day, 1 block south of the Court House in downtown Sport City.

REGISTRATION: Race day registration will be permitted from 6:15 until 7:30 a.m.

T-SHIRTS: All participants who register before Tuesday, June 5 will receive a Sport City T-Shirt.

AWARDS: Trophies will be given for the best overall times for men and women. Trophies will also be given to the 1st, 2nd and 3rd place finishers in each division.

AGE-DIVISIONS: MEN'S AND WOMEN'S DIVISIONS
    14 & under   15-20   21-29   40-49   50 & over

— —

COUNTRY FEDERAL LOAN OFFICIAL ENTRY FORM
10,000 METER RUN

One Entry Per Form — type or print

Name _____
    Last   First   Middle Initial

Age (Race Day) ____ Sex ____ Date of Birth _____

Street _____ City _____ State _____ Zip _____

Phone Number _____ Club Affiliation _____

In case of Emergency contact _____ Phone _____

T-Shirt Size—for those registering before June 5.
    Small ____ Medium ____ Large ____ X-Large ____

In consideration for the acceptance of my entry, I for myself, my executors, heirs and signees, do hereby release and discharge Country Federal Loan Association and the Road Runner Club, Sport City and the Parks and Recreation Department and other sponsors and supporters for all claims of damages, demands, actions whatsoever in any manner arising or growing out of my participating in said athletic event. I attest and verify that I have full knowledge of the risks involved in this event and I am physically fit and sufficiently trained to participate in this event.

_____ Return **Entry with remittance to:**
Date   Signature   Sport City Road Runner Club
                              P.O. Box 111
                              Sport City, Illinois 10001

_____

Date (if under 18, parent's signature)
— —

• Is there a reasonable explanation of the procedures?
• Is the participant asked to 'waive' a legal right through exculpatory language?
• Is the release clearly visible?
• Is such a form, as in this event, targeted more for the adult population?
• Is the intent of parent signature for those under 18 years of age to grant permission or "waive" their right?

Risk Management Suggestions

• The utilization of accident/injury reports will assist in identification of high risk areas where the use of a 'waiver' or 'informed consent' would be feasible.
• Community service programs involving the adult and/or senior learner are potential areas for the "waiver and release" format, depending upon the risk factor, condition of the participant, and other influencing parameters (insurance, medical compensation, etc.).
• All activity areas are suitable target areas for using 'informed consent' or 'waivers': Physical education, intramurals, athletics special events (thons of a wide variety, jog-a-thon, etc.) and individual sport activity.
• Teachers, coaches and administrators should become thoroughly acquainted with and be able to differentiate between the "waiver of release" and "informed consent" agreements, utilizing the appropriate concept for the most suitable situation.

- Prior to the start of the school year and/or during the planning of programs an assessment of potential risk areas, nature of involved populations, insurance, and medical compensation should be made to ascertain if, when, where and how a 'waiver' or 'informed consent' instrument will be used.
- Legal counsel should be used in the development of either instrument to assure conformity to legal guidelines, avoiding pitfalls and becoming a legally effective instrument. Remember these instruments are agreements and require strict construct and language.
- Consider the development of a comprehensive "informed consent" format which would focus on the program in toto and then shift to specific high risk activities.

  A possible format may include:
  1. *Letter* of Announcement and Invitation. All parents and students would be invited to a special meeting prior to the start of the school year.
  2. *Open Meeting* would be conducted to explain the program/activity philosophy general procedures, expected benefits, attendant risks, alternatives, and any disclaimers.
  3. *Visual* presentation, slides, video tape, or movie clip, covering the program and activity would be presented.

     Procedures - time, date, places, practices, training and development, competition, coaching methods, sports medicine care and expectation.

     Benefits (PROS) - physical, psychological, social and academic.

     Risks (CONS) - the least to the most catastrophic, not only the physical functional risk, but also the academic.

     Alternatives - withdraw voluntarily without biasness on the part of program personnel.

     Disclaimers - extent of responsibility for insurance and/or medical compensation by program and/or parent. Not exculpatory but informatory, it is an explanation of what will or what will not be provided by the school with regard to medical compensation and/or insurance.
  4. *Question and Answer* period by parents and students.
  5. *Letter and Signature*, a form is provided summarizing the presentation and key points which the parent and student are asked to sign, leave or be collected.

6. After school commences, the coaches in high risk sports, teachers or sponsors of special events would present a similar but modified program for their specific area:
   a. Letter of announcement
   b. Meeting showing a visual presentation *specific to the sport* or *activity* and covering procedures, benefits, risks, alternatives, disclaimers, etc.
   c. Questions and Answer
   d. Letter and signature.
7. Letters from the general and specific orientation programs should be retained on file.
8. Consideration in development should be given to some standardization of letters and computerization for facilitation, efficiency and storage.

- Storage of letters on microfiche or 35 mm slides would facilitate retention for recordkeeping purpose while minimizing bulk and space requirements.
- "Warning It Could Happen to You," Triad Films, Cedar Rapids, Iowa, or similar films are excellent modalities for helping the student make an "informed decision."

Selected References

Bowdoin College v. Cooper International 403 A 2d 1206.

Cebik, L.B., *The Review of Research Involving Human Subjects*, Chairman Committee on Research Participation, University of Tennessee, Report at Illinois State University, 1-22-81.

DeKalb v. White et al., 260 SE 2d 853.

Lynch v. Board of Education Collinsville, 390 NE 2d 526.

Poole v. South Plainfield Board of Education, 490 F Supp. 948.

Ross, Tom. "Waivers Release of Liability, Club Sport," *What You Don't Know Can Hurt You*, Law and Sports Conference, 1984, p.98.

Weistart, J.C., Lowell, C.H. *The Law of Sports*, Bobbs-Merrill Co., Indianapolis, 1979, p. 964.

45 *Code of Federal Regulations* 46.103C

CHAPTER X
A Learning Experience

The study of law in sport and physical activity has gained in popularity. One need only to review textbooks in administration and management since 1960 to discover the increased interest and emphasis on the topic. Additionally, since the early 1970's, there has been an increase in the number of books on the specific topic, books not necessarily limited to the legal professional.

Conferences, seminars, short courses and convention sessions on law and activity are now standard operating procedure. The Indiana University School of Law on August 20, 1981 initiated one of the first conferences focused on law and amateur sports. And, it is now possible to find sample curricular models for establishing a class in law and sports. Some excellent curriculum and instructional suggestions are presented by Nancy N. Mathews on page 200 in *Sports and the Courts*, "Physical Education and Sports Law Quarterly," Guilford College, Greensboro, North Carolina, June 6-10, 1983.

As early as the summer of 1968, a workshop on the legal aspects of physical education and sport was conducted at Illinois State University. And, there has been a constant attempt to provide quality learning experiences through case reports, book reviews, guest lecturers, and social problem/conflict identification.

An excellent group exercise can be structured using a court room model (Hicks). The 'mock court' model is composed of five (5) basic components which may be adapted and modified according to class size. In this instance class size for the example is 19 students. And, the components are:
1. Justices
2. Chief Justice
3. Timer-Recorder
4. Appellee [defendant]
5. Appellant [plaintiff]
   Observers (optional)

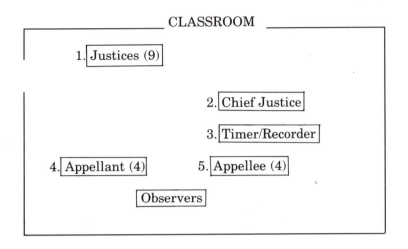

CLASSROOM

1. Justices (9)

2. Chief Justice

3. Timer/Recorder

4. Appellant (4)   5. Appellee (4)

Observers

Group membership and individual role may be established by blind draw, ballot, volunteering or appointment by the instructor. Every attempt should be made to assure the interactive nature of the various components. The experience is culminated by a summative session by the instructor, which is done following a distribution of all materials to all members of the class.

Functionally, the group learning experience would center on a case selected by the instructor for its 'troubled' nature in the profession, essential risk components, points of law and potential as a living learning experience. Facts and issues would be gleaned from the report of the case and prepared as four [4] separate distributions. Each preparation would include a description of the case and then the essentials peculiar to each group. Using Lantz v. Amach [620 F.Supp.663] as a sample case, this would provide an opportunity to discuss issues of Sex Discrimination, Title IX, Federal Funding Strategies, Grove City decision. The case centered on a female who wanted to play football.

Appellant [plaintiff] and appellee [defendant] groups are provided the facts of the case appropriate to their position. And, they are provided a sufficient amount of time (about seven minutes) to organize a rationale in support of their position. The rationale must contain the essential facts and issues of the case; however, the groups are encouraged to embellish and expand into related issues for the sake of interaction. Beyond the citing and description the plaintiff [appellant] and defendant [appellee] would receive facts essential to their position: [Distribution 1 & 2]

Plaintiff LANTZ V. AMACH 620 F. SUPP. 663 **(description)	Defendant LANTZ V. AMACH 620 F. SUPP. 633 **(description)
Points for discussion:	Points for discussion:
1. She has an interest to try out.	1. Regulation blocks her attempt from the state Board of Regents, Board of Education, Commissioner and NYS Public H.S. Athletic Association.
2. The regulation is too broad and general.	
3. Where a girl is as fit or more to be on squad than the weakest of squad's male member. She should be entitled.	2. Rule: "There shall be no mixed competition in the following sports: basketball, boxing, football, ice hockey, rugby, and wrestling.
4. She would be assuming the risk of injury as male students do.	3. Defendant merely alleges on information and belief that H.S. receives funds.
5. There is no team for the plaintiff to try out for. [football].	4. The regulation which requires opportunity for females to try for male teams [or vice versa] where there is no team for their own sex does not apply here with contact football.
6. From what we hear and believe the program receives federal financial assistance.	
7. Excluding qualified member of one gender because they are presumed to suffer from inherent handicaps or to be inferior.	5. Object is to protect the health and safety of female students. [a] as a general rule, senior H.S. [15-18] are more physically developed, stronger, more agile, faster, greater muscular endurance than their female counterpart. [b] medical opposition to girls in contact sport because of risk of injury.

Justices raise questions developed upon a review of the preparation of facts and issues provided for them as a distribution [no. 3]. Similarly, they use the seven minutes to prepare their questions. And, as the facts are presented by the appellant and appellee, the justices listen for cues to raise questions. Their inquiry is interjected by saying "counselor" during rationale presentations. [Distribution 3]

DISTRIBUTION 3 — For the Justices

Lantz v. Amach [Individually and as Commissioner, New York State Department of Education and NYSPHAA]

620 F. SUPP. 663

A female student in her junior year at High School, who wanted to play football at school without a girls' football team. Public regulation prohibited mixed sex competition in football and other specified sports.
   —is the objective to protect?
   —is the regulation too broad and general?
   —is it fair to exclude qualified members of one sex while all
      others of another sex not as qualified are allowed to
      participate?

Listen to the plaintiff and defendant, raise questions, caucus and then announce your decision. It can be made in the form of the 1] assenting opinion, 2] major and dissenting opinion [3 to 2, or 4 to 3], in favor of the plaintiff or the defendant.
**

Discussion summation will follow after the ruling.

After the initial presentation by each side, a period of three minutes is allotted for each side to present a rebuttal to the points made in the position statement, which would constitute their final argument.

Justices caucus for a vote and announce the opinion of the group. It may be reported as the affirming and/or dissenting opinion. [Distribution 3]

The timer and recorder monitors and controls the various time segments: rationale of position seven (7) minutes each plus organizing time, rebuttal period is about six (6) minutes, three (3) each for the plaintiff and defendant, and the time for justices to caucus and present dissenting and/or affirming opinion (flexible factor).

Chief justice (instructor) attempts to direct the experience by focusing on cues about the case which may be amplified upon as they relate to the profession, risks, and points of law. Amplification and stressing points during the interrogative phase is essential to learning and the classroom atmosphere. Cue recognition is critical to the exercise. The culminating summation is essential to reinforce cognitive factors to be learned, to separate the embellished trends or emphasize a point. A final distribution is made and all students now have the case for discussion and summation: [Distribution 4]

DISTRIBUTION 4 — RULING ON CASE

LANTZ V. AMACH [Individually and as Commissioner, New York State Department of Education and NYSPFAA]
620 F. SUPP. 663

A female student in her junior year at High School, who wanted to play football at a school without a girl's football team. Public regulation prohibited mixed sex competition in football and other specified sports.

The defendant is ordered to:

1. defendants et al be restrained from refusing Jackie Lantz from participating on the J.V. Football squad on the same basis as males are allowed to compete.
2. determine plaintiff's eligibility pursuant to standards applied to all male condidates, and if eligible, she be permitted to try out.
3. permanently restrained and enjoined from taking action against any plaintiff or defendant because of their compliance herewith, or from interfering with Jackie's opportunity so long as she is eligible.

In a large class a section of observers may be created to generate discussion and direction during a post-evaluation phase of the group exercise. A test on cognitive content could be conducted immediately after the exercise or at a subsequent class or at the end of the unit.

Although the 'mock court' is quite flexible, it is best suited for classes which are eight (8) or more in enrollment. Its success is dependent upon the directive or non-directive skill of the lead teacher to generate and maintain interaction as a resultant of identified cues. Undoubtedly, the selection of the case, preplanning and orienting the class are important to the success of the experience.

Learning in this context can be enjoyable and exciting.

Course Syllabus

Course Title: LEGAL ASPECTS OF SPORT AND PHYSICAL
EDUCATION. 3 semester hours. Spring and summer.

Course Description: Identification of problems, trends, and implications for Sport and Physical Education through
a study of statutory law and ruling case law.

Objectives:

The student will:

1. demonstrate a working knowledge of legal research techniques
by writing case reports.
2. identify and analyze human and environmental factors in
sports and physical education, relating to play as a process.
3. study specific aspects of injury with the intent of identifying
controls designed to minimize accidents, risks, and/or hazards.
4. identify plaintiff behavior patterns and their implications for
responsible legal conduct.
5. identify social change, naked force, troubled cases and behavioral patterns in Sports and Physical Education which
necessitates legal action.

Outline of the Course:

   I. Research and the Law
     A. Schoolman in the Law Library
     B. Historical Research Techniques
       1. Primary Sources
       2. Secondary Sources
     C. Resource Materials
       1. American Jurisprudence
       2. Corpus Juris Seccendiem
       3. National Reporter System
       4. Digest System

  II. Nature of the Law
     A. Sources of Law
       1. Constitutional
       2. Statutory
       3. Case
     B. Purposes of Law
       1. Social
       2. Functional

C. Significant Principles and Concepts
  1. Liability
  2. Duty
  3. Negligence
  4. Proximate Cause
  5. Tort
  6. Defenses
D. Primitive Law

III. Selected Topics
A. Regulation of Amateur Athletics
B. Public Regulating of Sports Activities
C. Legal Relationships in Professional Sports
D. Liability for Injuries in Sports Activities
E. Enforcement of Contracts
F. Antitrust Aspects
G. The Team Physician
H. Sports Equipment
I. Sports Medicine Personnel
J. Research Techniques and the Laboratory
K. Supervision
L. Handicapped Performers

IV. Organizational Factors
A. Risk Management
B. Supervisory Principles
C. Due Process Concepts
D. Emergency Procedures and Accident Reporting System
E. Insurance

Learning Experiences:

1. Individual Projects - Students will select a particular problem or topic and develop a case report utilizing research techniques.
2. Group Project - Each student will serve on two committees to develop a solution to a problem area by identifying the forces and issues as related to the problem.
3. Guest speakers with expertise in problem areas and/or law will provide clarification and understanding for the students.

Text(s) and Readings:

*No required text

Readings:

Legal Resources

American Digest System, West Publishing Co., St. Paul, Minn.,
    Century Digest, Vol. 43, 1903, cases 1658 to 1896.
    First Decennial Digest, Vol. 16, 1910, cases 1897 to 1906.
    Second Decennial Digest, Vol. 20, 1922, cases 1906 to 1916.
    Third Decennial Digest, Vol. 24, 1929, cases 1916 to 1926.
    Fourth Decennial Digest, Vol. 27, 1938, cases 1926 to 1936.
    Fifth Decennial Digest, Vol. 39, 1949, cases 1936 to 1946.
    Sixth Decennial Digest, Vol. 26, 1958, cases 1946 to 1956.

American Jurisprudence, Lawyer's Co-operative Publishing Co.,
    Rochester, N.Y.

American Law Reports, Lawyer's Co-operative Publishing Co.,
    Rochester, N.Y. (Annual) 1919.

Black's Law Dictionary, West Publishing Co., 4th Edition, St.
    Paul, Minn., 1951.

Corpus Juris, American Law Book Co., New York. (Wm. Mock)

Corpus Juris Secundum, American Law Book Co., New York.
    (F.J. Luder & H.J. Gilbert).

National Reporter System, West Publishing Co., St. Paul, Minn.
    (weekly)

(The) Atlantic Reporter - Decisions 1885 to date (courts of last
    resort); Connecticut, Delaware, Maryland, New Hampshire,
    New Jersey, Pennsylvania, Rhode Island, Vermont.

California Reporter - Decisions 1959 to date in California Supreme
    Court and lower courts.

Federal Reporter - U.S. District Court and U.S. Circuit Court
    decisions 1880 to date.

Federal Supplement - U.S. District Court decisions since 1932,
    Court of Claims 1932 to 1960, U.S. Customs Court 1949 to
    date.

New York Supplement - cases of New York Court of Appeals and
    lower courts, 1888 to date.

North Eastern Reporter - Decisions 1885 to date, courts of last
    resort: Illinois, Indiana, Massachuset, New York, Ohio.

Northwestern Reporter - Decisions 1879 to date, courts of last
    resort: Iowa, Michigan, Minnesota, Nebraska, North Dakota,
    South Dakota, Wisconsin.

Pacific Reporter - Decisions 1833 to date, courts of last resort:
    Alaska, Arizona, California, Colorado, Hawaii, Idaho, Kansas,
    Montana, Nevada, New Mexico, Oklahoma, Oregon, Utah,
    Washington, Wyoming.

South Western Reporter - Decisions 1886 to date, courts of last resort: Arkansas, Kentucky, Missouri, Tennessee, Texas.

Southern Reporter - Decisions 1887 to date, courts of last resort: Alabama, Florida, Louisiana, Mississippi.

Supreme Court Reporter - Decisions 1882 to date of the U.S. Supreme Court.

Books

Alexander, K. and Soloman, E., *College and University Law*, the Michie Company, Charlottesville, Virginia, 1972.

Appenzeller, H., *Physical Education and the Law*, the Michie Company, Charlottesville, Virginia, 1972.

Appenzeller, H., *Physical Education and the Law*, the Michie Company, Charlottesville, Virginia, 1978.

Bryson, J.E. and Beutley, C.P., *Ability Grouping of Public School Students,* the Michie Company, Charlottesville, Virginia, 1980.

Decof, L., Godosky, R., *Sports Injury Litigation,* Practicing Law Institute, New York, N.Y., 1979.

Hudgins, H.C., and Vacca, R.S., *Law and Education: Contemporary Issues and Court Decisions,* the Michie Company, Charlottesville, Virginia, 1979.

Evaluation:

Students will be evaluated on their:

1. Individual projects which will reflect their writing and research skill and constitute 20%.
2. Group projects (2) and will constitute 10% of the grade to total 20%.
3. Presentation (oral) of the case report in relationship to social change, troubled cases, naked force or behavioral patterns will constitute 20%. Peer evaluation will judge the quality of individual defense of issues.
4. Quizzes of cognitive content to constitute 20%.
5. Final examination to constitute 20% of the grade.

Selected References

Hicks, R., *Attorney at Law,* Golden Valley, Minn., April, 1986, Normal, IL.

Koehler, Robert W. Course Syllabus, Illinois State University, Normal, IL, July, 1986.

CHAPTER XI
Research and Resources

Research

Generally, it is difficult for the teacher to motivate students to have an interest in pure research. Often the practical aspects of research seem to elude the students. Or, they fail to see its application to the job. It is perceived as a programmatic necessity to receive a degree and get on with the job.

However, there are a multitude of realities necessitating staying abreast of the law, conflict and social climate. The so called "deep pocket" theory has contributed to the escalation of recovery amounts, legal fees and insurance premiums. Product liability has been an attrition factor within in the sporting goods industry, especially in relation to the manufacture of football helmets.

The "tort crisis" of the 1980's has resulted in the elimination of liability insurance as an employee benefit by some agencies, institutions and businesses. Because of ballooning premiums, there have been organizational funds, or alternative sources formed to service employees in case of a litigation.

Additionally, some parks and recreational areas have removed hazardous equipment, established more restrictive hours or closed their doors in order to control insurance cost factors and manage risk potential.

Insurance companies have reassessed their position relative to underwriting liability coverage. The course of action has ranged from more restrictive policy language to opting out of the liability insurance market.

These realities should be sufficient for the professional in play and sport activity to be tuned to the current social trends and needs in a legal sense. The law has responded to equal opportunity for all to participate, dress code, eligibility, child abuse, due process, pupil injury, tenure, employment and a variety of other situations. But where does one start to be informed about the legal aspects of physical activity and the profession?

To start, a determination should be made as to whether it is the law (statutes) to be examined or the "state of the art" as opinioned by authorities. The legal status, conflict and social problems may be gleaned from a variety of periodicals and/or journals authored by various authorities. The law, statutory and ruling case law, will only be available through a variety of primary and secondary sources in the law, accessible through the law reference system.

General articles about law, results and implications of the law, or "state of the art" discussion about the legal aspects of physical activity are readily available in most all libraries. On the other hand, the law reference system may be limited to very large libraries, courthouses with law libraries, Bar associations, large insurance companies, and universities, especially those with a law school.

Irrespective of the library, there are some resource materials or tools which will facilitate the teacher-coach in locating essential information sources:

1. *Readers Guide to Periodical Literature:* articles in magazines and journals found by topic and title. Most indexes run approximately six weeks to over six months behind the appearance of the magazine. Other indexes are *Social Science Index, Popular Periodical Index, Magazine Index* and newspaper indexes.

2. *Physical Education Index:* A subject index to domestic and foreign periodicals in English or containing summaries in English. Each article is indexed in depth with no limit to the number of subject headings under which it is classified. Alphabetical topics or subjects may lead to: title, author, name of periodical, volume, inclusive pages, month and year article was published.

3. *Educational Resource Information Center (ERIC):* A national information system, designed and supported by the United States Office of Education, for providing ready access to information that can be used in developing more effective educational programs. Steps are Thesaurus of Descriptors, Subject Index Resume of Studies, Microfiche of complete study, Extend to other periodicals.

4. Dialog File 150 and the *Legal Resource Index:* a special focus program utilizing descriptors to yield information from law sources; 1980-present, 194,500 records, monthly updates (Information Access Company, Belmont, CA). LEGAL RESOURCE INDEX provides cover-to-cover indexing of over 750 key law journals and 6 law newspapers plus legal monographs. The LEGAL RESOURCE INDEX comprehensively

indexes articles, book reviews, case notes, president's pages, columns, letters to the editor, obituaries, transcripts, biographical pieces, and editorials providing access to valuable secondary information for the legal profession and others. Relevant law articles from MAGAZINE INDEX (File 47), NATIONAL NEWSPAPER INDEX (File 111) and TRADE AND INDUSTRY INDEX (File 148) are also included.

5. Dialog File 35: Comprehensive Dissertation Abstracts: Another Lockheed corporation program which utilizes descriptors to find completed dissertations on the law, sport and physical education.

6. Lexis: A computerized case-finding system owned by Mead Data Central corporation. This enables one to search the full text of recent cases and statutes in special libraries of materials.

LEXIS

Subject: Law

Summary: Largest on-line, full-text database of legal information. Incorporates libraries of federal law (general, tax, security, trade regulations, patent/trademark/ copyright, communications, labor bankruptcy, energy, public contacts); state law libraries; U.K. and French law libraries; and other services (Auto-Cite, Shepard Citations, Matthew Bender treaties). See also LEXPAT.

Corresponding Printed Sources: Publications of Matthew Bender & Co., (ex. Kheel on labor Law, Shepard's Citations (McGraw-Hill) Auto-Cite (Lawyers Cooperative Publishing Co.)

Time Coverage: File Size: LEXIS is part of Mead Daa Central's database which had 63.8 billion characters and 14.2 million document as of Dec. 9, 1983. NEXIS is also part of this database.

Vendor and Price Information: Mead Data Central, prices vary widely; depending on volume; contact Mead for further details on surcharges, monthly library access, monthly equipment and one-time charges (terminal installation/move charges) and instruction fees. Telecommunication charges are included in above fees.

Language: English, French public and private case law, statutes, regulations etc. in French.

Restrictions/Conditions: subscription required, available only in U.S., France, U.K.

Accessed Through: MeadNet, Telenet, direct dial; not available in Canada or Mexico.

Search Aids Available: user manuals free for subscribers, database documentation free for subscribers.

7. Westlaw: West Publishing Company system is a full text system, including synapses and headnotes. West Publishing, St. Paul, Minnesota.

8. American Digest System: A master index system consisting of the Centuri Edition (1658-1896), Decennial Digests (1897-1975) all but the first covering ten year periods with 1976-1986 in progress, and monthly pamphlets and annual General Digest to update the series.

9. Computer: It is wise for the researcher to be acquainted with technology systems of the specific library. Most libraries are technologically advanced to provide searches of their in house volumes. These systems are time savers and usually cost free.

A word of caution. The technologically advanced systems are not a panacea to the search, finding all the available information. The computer is but an aid. It is an aid that contains only those items it has been programmed to contain. A combination of techniques may in fact be more successful in uncovering a depth of essential material.

The functional efficiency of most of the systems is dependent upon the use of abbreviations, topics, descriptors, key phrases or key numbering systems. Descriptors which have been used in ERIC are: Tort, Negligence, Liability, Sports, Physical Education, Recreation, Injury, Athletics, Athletes, Pupil, Public Education, Primary Education, Secondary Education, or a combination of these descriptors, the search may be limited to a time period, i.e. 1980-82, specific program, or both. The cost of such a search may be according to search time and prints per selected descriptors.

When embarking upon research of the law, it is important to know what each legal tool provides within legal research. Research on the law, statutory and case, is possible through a reference system which provides both primary and secondary sources. These tools deal with specific areas in the law and are functionally different, depending on outlines, topics, titles, names, cases, key numbers, abbreviations and cross references. These tools are:

Constitutions - Federal appears in the United States Code. State Constitution included in each latest state code.

State Statutes - State codes of general laws should be used instead of or in connection with state departments of education compilation. Ammendments would be found with the code.

Shepard's Citation to Statutes - Enables one to find out what has happened to the statute. Merely a listing of numbers and abbreviations which tells what has happened.

State Law Index - available up to 1949, after 1949 Library of Congress suspended funding. It was a compilation of state legislation by subject matter. Now each state must be researched separately.

Court Decisions - Most states have "reports," state reports of cases, i.e. *ILL. App.*

American Digest System - Used to build a bibliography of cases. Consists of Century Edition and Dicennial Digest. Has three parts: a listing by topic, a table of cases, and a descriptive word index to facilitate selection of the particular term or topic for identification.

National Reporter System - All cases from all courts of record, actual opinion of the courts. 9 geographical divisions: Southern Reporter, Southwestern Reporter, Southeastern Reporter, Pacific Reporter, Northwestern Reporter, Northeastern Reporter, Atlantic Reporter, Supreme Court Reporter and Federal Reporter.

Volumes are numbered consecutively for the years in the series, 1st series (1 to), 2nd Series (1 to).

Annotated Reports - Seven (7) series, latest series is the A.L.R. which began in 1919, six volumes each year, only the leading cases, cases which are new or deal with questions on which there is conflict of legal opinion.

Shepard's Citation to Cases - A number and abbreviation system which tells whether there have been later cases; disapproved, modified or reversed. What has happened to the case. Other Shepard's exist: Shepard's to U.S. Citation, Shepard's Federal Citation, Shepard's Illinois Citation, they all tell what has happened to the law or cases.

Corpus Juris Secundum - C.J.S. all inclusive cases around a principle in law in encyclopedia form.

American Jurisprudence - ruling case law in encyclopedia for containing only leading cases.

Although the computer will make most efficient use of time and volume, it is also possible to facilitate the library search by utilizing certain topics and key numbers. In order to read case opinion on a selected topic the American Digest System is used to build a bibliography of cases. It is the master index of American case law; and, covers all reported cases from 1658 to the present time:

American Digest System, West Publishing Co., St. Paul, MN
Century Digest, Vol. 43, 1903, cases 1658 to 1896.
First Decennial Digest, Vol. 17, 1910, cases 1897 to 1906.
Second Decennial Digest, Vol. 20, 1922. cases 1906 to 1916.
Third Decennial Digest, Vol. 24, 1929, cases 1916 to 1926.
Fourth Decennial Digest, Vol. 27, 1938, cases 1926 to 1936.
Fifth Decennial Digest, Vol. 39, 1949, cases 1936 to 1946.
Sixth Decennial Digest, Vol. 26, 1958, cases 1946 to 1956
Seventh Decennial Digest, 1956 to 1966.
Eighth Decennial Digest, 1966 to 1976.

The digest contains legal and non-legal terms, many cross references, a synopsis of a key topic and a key number. Reading the brief key synopsis, the research can decide whether the case in its entirety should be read. It is only the court opinion from case reports that may be cited. The holding of a case cannot be cited on the basis of the digest alone.

Cases within each of the units related to "Schools and School Districts" may be identified by reviewing the topical outline, selecting the key numbered item and then locating the key number in the volume:

Key 147, Duties and Liabilities from the subject matter outline "Schools and School Districts" will yield all reported cases for the given period of time for review and selection. If a case is selected, the digest summary provides a cross reference case citing for locating the case in the appropriate National Reporter.

Key numbers in the American Digest System of particular importance are:
88   Liabilities specially imposed by statute
89.2 Negligence in general
89.3 Particular torts in general
89.4 Athletics and Physical Education
89.7 Injuries to persons other than pupils
89.9 _____ Contributory negligence
89.11Supervision of other pupils
89.12_____ Play and recess

The topical outline in the Digest is entitled "Schools", followed by subjects included therein and a three point outline with many keyed subdivisions:
I.   Private Schools and Academies
II. Public Schools
III. Interscholastic Associations

The previously listed key numbered items are subdivisions of II. Public Schools.

Once having identified a case citing from he Digest System, i.e. 172 N.E. 19, the case may be read in the reporter system. The National Reporter System contains reports of the highest courts in every state grouped by geographical area. The Reporter System also incorporates Supreme Court cases, cases from the U.S. Court of Appeals, and cases from the U.S. District Courts. Federal Rules Decisions contains cases which focus on procedural matters before the courts:

National Reporter System, West Publishing Co., St. Paul, Minn. (weekly)

(The) Atlantic Reporter - Decisions 1885 to date (courts of last resort): Connecticut, Delaware, Maryland, New Hampshire, New Jersey, Pennsylvania, Rhode Island, Vermont.

California Reporter - Decisions 1959 to date in California Supreme Court and lower courts.

Federal Reporter - U.S. Districts Court and U.S. Circuit Court decisions 1880 to date.

Federal Supplement - U.S. DIstrict Court decisions since 1932, Court of Claims 1932 to 1960, U.S. Customs Court 1949 to date.

New York Supplement - cases of New York Court of Appeals and lower courts, 1888 to date.

North Eastern Reporter - Decisions 1885 to date, courts of last resort: Illinois, Indiana, Massachusetts, New York, Ohio.

Northwestern Reporter - Decisions 1879 to date, courts of last resort: Iowa, Michigan, Minnesota, Nebraska, North Dakota, South Dakota, Wisconsin.

Pacific Reporter - Decisions 1833 to date, courts of last resort: Alaska, Arizona, California, Colorado, Hawaii, Idaho, Kansas, Montana, Nevada, New Mexico, Oklahoma, Oregon, Utah, Washington, Wyoming.

South Eastern Reporter - Decisions 1887 to date, courts of last resort: Georgia, North Carolina, South Carolina, Virginia, West Virginia.

South Western Reporter - Decisions 1886 to date, courts of last resort: Arkansas, Kentucky, Missouri, Tennessee, Texas.

Southern Reporter - Decisions 1887 to date, courts of last resort: Alabama, Florida, Louisiana, Mississippi.

Supreme Court Reporter - Decisions 1882 to date of the U.S. Supreme Court.

Shepard's Reporter Citations, Shepard's Citations, Inc., Colorado Springs, Colorado.

State Reports - Decisions in full in the courts of record in each state.

United States Reports - Decisions since 1790 to date of the Supreme Court of the U.S.

Series Name	Abbreviation
Pacific	P.
North Western	N.W.
North Eastern	N.E.
Atlantic	A.
South Eastern	S.E.
South Western	S.W.
Southern	So.
California Reporter	Cal.Rep.
New York Supplement	N.Y.S.
Federal Rules Decisions	F.R.D.
Federal Supplement	F.Supp.
Federal Reporter	F.
Supreme Court Reporter	S.Ct.

In all regional Reporters, there are two series. The first series has no identification on the book spine below the title; the second series is identified by "2d" on the spine. Being familiar with the functional nature of the Digest System and National Reporter System, the student can find cases to read around legal topics and social problems. And, if a person has access to 'Lexis' and/or 'Westlaw' case-finding can be greatly shortened. This search does not make for scholarly research but it does facilitate the educator in the law library. For the more serious legal scholar and research, a person should become familiar with legal materials such as:

Price, Miles O. and Harry Bitner. *Effective Legal Research.* Textbook format that includes basis reference tools and methods of legal research.

Rezny, Arthur A. and M. K. Remmlein. *A Schoolman in the Law Library.* Problems, bibliography, research tools, cases analysis and glossary in a booklet format.

Roalfe, William R. *How to Find the Law.* Comprehensive guidelines and instructions on how to use the tools of legal research.

Resources

A review of the search systems and their components will help to emphasize the facilitory nature of the technology.

During participation in the International Symposium for Comparative Physical Education and Sport (1986), Vancouver, British Columbia, it was convenient to visit their School of Law and review some materials. The librarian utilized their in-house computer and programs with a general request for books on "*Sports and Law*." The run time was less than one minute with no cost to the user and a yield of eleven resources. It was and is a service to the student.

1. Berry, Robert C.
   Law and business of the sports industries.
   Boston, MA, Auburn House Pub. Co. 1986.
2. Yasser, Raymond L.
   Torts and sports: legal liability in professional and amateur athletics.
   Westport Quorum Books, 1985.
3. Sport, physical activity and the law/Raymond et.al.
   Vanier, Out Canadian Association for Health, Physical Education 1985.
4. Sports violence and law reform.
   Ottawa Carleton University: Dept. of Law 1985.
5. Berry, Robert C.
   Labor relations in professional sports/Robert C. Berry, et.al.
   Cambridge, MA, Ballinger Publishing Co. 1985.
6. Uberstine, Gary A.
   Covering all the bases: a comprehensive research guide to sports law.
   Buffalo, NY Hein 1985.
7. Great Britain. Committee of inquiry into crowd safety and control at sports grounds.
   Interim report
   London HMSO, 1985.
8. Yasser, Raymond L.
   Sports law: cases and materials
   Lanham, MD Univ. Pr of America 1985
9. European anti-doping charter for sports: recommendation no. R(84)19 . . .
   Strasbourg Council of Europe 1985
10. Riffen, Jeffery K.
    Sports and recreational injuries
    Colorado Springs Shepard's/McGraw Hill 1985.

11. Redhead, S.C.
Policing the field: legal interventions in professional football.
Coventry University of Warwick 1986.

An ERIC search utilizing DIALOG FILE 35: Completed Dissertation Abstracts was estimated to cost $4.80. It yielded forty-six resource items for examination in a matter of minutes.

1. Tort liability of organized camps for children: a study of case law. 251 pages.
Fowler, Susan Lynn (Ed.D. 1981 University of Georgia).
Page 1312 in volume 42/03-a of dissertation abstracts international.
Recreation

2. State and municipal government tort liability for parks and recreation services in the United States. 229 pages.
Schultz, John Herbert (Ph.D. 1968 University of Minnesota).
Page 2130 in volume 29/07a of Dissertation Abstracts International.
Education, recreation

3. An analysis of court cases pertaining to tort liability for injuries sustained in a public school program of physical education. 187 pages.
Appenzeller, Herbert Thomas (Ed.D. 1966 Duke University).
Page 1570 in volume 27/06-a of Dissertation Abstracts International.
Education, administration

4. Analysis of tort liability of school districts and/or its officers, agents, and employees in conducting programs of physical education, recreation, and athletics. 259 pages.
Soich, John E. (Ed.D. 1964 University of Pittsburgh).
Page 182 in volume 26/01 of Dissertation Abstracts International.
Education, administration

5. Tort law: negligence and liability in physical education with reference to higher education. 241 pages.
Stremlau, Duane L. (Ph.D. 1976 The University of Wisconsin-madison).
Page 158 in volume 38/01-a of Dissertation Abstracts International.
Education, physical

6. An analysis of court cases pertaining to tort liability of teachers for injuries sustained by pupils in school programs of physical education and of the eroding doctrine of immunity of school districts. 290 pages.
   Carley, John Mitchell (Ed.D. 1976 University of Houston).
   Page 4732 in volume 37/08-a of Dissertation Abstracts International.
   Education, administration
7. An investigation of the knowledge of tort liability among chief personnel officers in the southern college personnel association. 82 pages.
   Rhodes, Fred Wayne (Ed.D. 1980 Mississippi State University).
8. Trends in tort liability of trustees for student injuries in private institutions of higher education. 186 pages.
   Andberg, Wendy Louise (Ph.D. 1980 University of Minnesota).
9. The tort liability of school districts in Illinois. 413 pages.
   Bell, Stephen Clifford (Ed.D. 1979 University of Illinois at Urbana-Champaign).
10. Tort liability of public school districts, in selected states, as affected by either a common law or a statutory immunity. 252 pages.
    Torres, Antonio Ignatio (Ed.D. 1973 Loyola University of Chicago).
11. A comparison of costs incurred in non-injury automobile accidents under tort liability and no-fault reparation systems. 267 pages.
    Tenney, Lester Irwin (D.B.A. 1972 University of Southern California).
12. A study of tort liability and tort immunity of eleemosynary and public institutions of higher education. 153 pages.
    Slahor, Eugenia Charmaine (Ph.D. 1971 The University of Utah).
13. Tort liability of Georgia school districts, school boards, school officers and school employees. 297 pages.
    Scoggins, Alvin Earon, Jr. (Ed.D. 1970 University of Georgia).
14. Tort liability and accountability for corporal punishment by Utah classroom teachers.
    Wolfley, E. Scott (Ph.D. 1963 The University of Utah).
15. The philosophy and principles of tort and contractual liability of eleemosynary educational institutions.

Smith, William Walter (Ph.D. 1961 University of Portland).
16. The comparative status of school district liability for torts in Oklahoma, California, and New York as evidenced by reported court decisions and statutory enactments in these three states: to identify the principles of law affecting the tort liability of school districts in the states of Oklahoma, California, and New York and to compare the status of the three states to principles.
Moss, John R., Jr. (Ph.D. 1960 The University of Tulsa).
17. The status of governmental immunity as it applies to the tort liability of school districts for injuries to pupils.
Davis, Elaine Carsley (Ph.D. 1958 The Johns Hopkins University).
18. Tort liability of private schools and charitable institutions. 199 pages.
Page, William (Ph.D. 1952 Temple University).
19. Tort liability of school districts in the United States. 117 pages.
Fuller, Ernest E. (Ph.D. 1950 Harvard University).
20. Psychic injury and tort liability in New York. 343 pages.
McNiece, Harold F. (Ph.D. 1949 New York University).
21. Legal aspects of tort liability in school districts as indicated by recent court decisions. 400 pages.
Satterfield, Ted J. (Ph.D. 1949 Temple University).
22. The tort liability of individual employees and officers of school districts for damages
Dice, Clifford O. (Ph.D. 1937 University of Southern California).
23. A study of legal trends and school district liability experience for the purpose of predicting ultimate costs for school districts in Minnesota if tort immunity is abrograted on January 1, 1970. 439 pages.
Knaak, William C. (Ph.D. 1969 University of Minnesota).
24. Higher education: the tort liability risk and its treatment by institutions and individuals. 105 pages.
Anderson, Ronald T. (Ph.D. 1967 The Florida State University).
25. A study of the tort liability in selected proprietary functions of the colleges and universities in Tennessee. 190 pages.
England, Don Carmichael (Ed.D. 1968 Memphis State University.)
26. State and municipal government tort liability for parks and recreation services in the United States. 229 pages.

Schultz, John Herbert (Ph.D. 1968 University of Minnesota).
27. Liability in selected states with some implications for school district agents and employees. 120 pages.
Rowley, George A. (Ed.D. 1967 Oklahoma State University).
28. The vulnerability of school districts in New York State for tort liability in the employment of teacher aides. 233 pages.
Wetterer, Charles M. (Ed.D. 1967 New York University).
29. Governmental immunity and tort liability of public school districts in Michigan and selected states. 352 pages.
Sauerbrun, R. Adam (Ed.D. 1967 Wayne State University).
30. Recent trends in tort liability of public schools and implications for the public schools of Pennsylvania. 116 pages.
Boy, Edwin William (Ed.D. 1966 The Pennsylvania State University).
31. An analysis of court cases pertaining to tort liability for injuries sustained in a public school program of physical education. 187 pages.
Appenzeller, Herbert Thomas (Ed.D. 1966 Duke University).
32. Tort liability of public schools. 198 pages.
Lemley, Charles Ray (Ph.D. 1964 East Texas State University).
33. Analysis of tort liability of school districts and/or its officers, agents, and employees in conducting programs of physical education, recreation and athletics. 259 pages.
Soich, John E. (Ed.D. 1964 University of Pittsburgh).
34. The nonimmunity of school districts to tort liability. 217 pages.
Hartman, Robert Duane (Ed.D. 1963 University of Illinois at Urbana-Champaign).
35. A study of tort liability in Michigan school districts. 228 pages.
Wood, Lewis Chapman (Ed.D. 1962 Michigan State University).
36. Trends in tort liability of school districts as revealed by court decisions. 276 pages.
Martin, David Vance (Ed.D. 1962 Duke University).
37. Relationships of school board practices to tort liability immunity in selected Ohio schools. 282 pages.
Southard, Thomas Berton (Ph.D. 1962 The Ohio State University).
38. Tort liability of colleges and universities. 213 pages.
Pittillo, Robert Albert, Jr. (Ed.D. 1961 Duke University).

39. Tort liability affecting shop teachers with provisions for avoiding accidents and litigation. 240 pages.
Kigin, Denis John (Ed.D 1959 University of Missouri-Columbia).

40. The tort liability status of Indiana public schools and the current liability insurance practices of Indiana public school corporations. 301 pages.
Schaerer, Robert Warren (Ed.D. 1959 Indiana University).

41. An assessment of teachers' knowledge of and attitude toward tort liability in selected Iowa school districts. 190 pages.
Bembry, Deborah Elaine (Ph.D. 1978 The University of Iowa).

42. The potential tort liability of California public high school band directors.
Young, Malcolm Williamson (Ed.D. 1978 University of Southern California).

43. An analysis of court decisions pertaining to tort liability for student injuries sustained in science activities in public school systems throughout the United States. 152 pages.
Barrett, Harvey Benton (Ed.D. 1977 Virginia Polytechnic Institute and State University).

44. Tort law: negligence and liability in physical education with reference to higher education 241 pages.
Stremlau, Duane L. (Ph.D. 1976 The University of Wisconsin-Madison).

45. An analysis of court cases pertaining to tort liability of teachers for injuries sustained by pupils in school programs of physical education and of the eroding doctrine of immunity of school districts. 290 pages.
Carley, John Mitchell (Ed.D. 1976 University of Houston).

46. Tort liability and higher education: developmental analysis, synthesis, and contemporary status. 176 pages.
Tarbert, Jeffrey Jon (Ed.D. 1976 The George Washington University).

Another data system provides even more information essential to the legal researcher or law scholar at the outset, this is DIALOG FILE 150: Legal Resource Index. A cost projection for the following information was $17.19, 0.191 hrs FILE 150, 27 Descriptors, $1.15 TYMNET, $12.60, 13 prints, $20.94 estimated cost to yield:

Governmental immunity of school districts and their employees.

Berry, Nazar; Hysni, Blair
Mich. B.J. 60 80 (9) Feb 1981
portrait
JURISDICTION: Michigan
DESCRIPTORS: tort liability of school districts-analysis; school
districts-privileges and immunities; teachers-legal status,
laws, etc.; school employees-legal status, laws, etc.

School board liability for violations of federal rights.
Smith, Michael R.
Sch. L. Bull. 12 1(12) Jan 1981
JURISDICTION: United States
Monell v. Department of Social Services, 436 U.S. 658 (1978);
Owen v. City of Independence, 48 U.S.L.W. 4389 (1980); Maine
v. Thiboutot, 48 U.S.L.W. 4859 (1980)
DESCRIPTORS: privileges and immunities-cases; negligence-
cases; tort liability of school distrcits-cases; liability for school
accidents-cases.

Sovereign immunity: application of Missouri's 1978 sovereign im-
munity legislation to school districts. (case note)
Bay, Jeffrey S.
Mo. L. Rev. 45 771-784 Fall 1980
ARTICLE TYPE: case note
JURISDICTION: Missouri
Beiser v. Parkway School District, 589 S.W 2d 277 (Mo. 1979)
DESCRIPTORS: tort liability of school districts-cases; liability
for school accidents-cases; government liability-cases.

School held liable for sexual assualt on woman student. (Hastings
College of the Law)
Carrizosa, Philip
L.A. Daily J. v93 p1 July 31, 1980
col 2 028 col in.
JURISDICTION: California
NAMED PEOPLE: Siciliano, Loretta-litigation
DESCRIPTORS: California, University of. Hastings College of
the Law-litigation; tort liability of universities and colleges-
litigation

School district liability for injuries to truants. (case note)
Harutanian, Albert T., III
Calif. L. Rev. 68 881-894 July 198
ARTICLE TYPE: case note
JURISDICTION: California

Conway, F.J. "Who's Liable?" *Safety Education,* 2:3-4, Oct., 1960.

A basic vagueness in liability: profit making school is liable for all acts; charitable organizations seem to be court protected.

Dzenowagis, J.A. "An Accident Reporting System, Why Bother?" *Journal of Health, Physical Education and Recreation,* 33:24, February, 1962

An accident reporting system may fulfill moral and legal responsibility of safeguarding the student athlete.

Fahr, S.M. "Legal Liability for Athletic Injuries," *Journal of the National Athletic Trainers Association,* Miami Beach, Florida, P. 1-3, June, 1958.

Tort Liability - Vicarious Liability or Respondent Superior and available defenses.

Garber, Lee O., "Schoolman Can be Sued When Students Ride in His Car," *Nation's Schools,* December 4, 1963.

The Delaware "Guest Law" - Any nonpaying guest who rides in a car cannot sue for damages, unless the driver causes the accident intentionally.

Garber, L.O. "School District Liability," *American Association of School Administrators Bulletin,* Oct., 1953.

Governmental Immunity of School Districts as established by common law has been altered by some state legislatures.

Garber, L.O. "The Case of the Negligent Coach," *The Nations' Schools,* 59:77-79, May, 1957.

Public sentiment may be promoted through newspaper coverage in emergency situations. There is no standard of evaluating behavior in these situations.

Garber, L.O. "Upholds Authority of High School Athletic Association," *Nations Schools,* 65:61, June, 1960.

Garrison, C. "Have You Acted Negligently Today?" *Athletic Journal,* p. 10, December, 1958.

The teacher must act in a reasonable and prudent manner: Owed a duty, failed to observe the duty, injury occurred, proximate cause must be proven.

Gold, S.Y. "First Aid and Legal Liability," *Journal of Health, Physical Education and Recreation,* 34:42-3, Jan., 1963.

A prescribed first aid procedure is necessary for the legal protection of the P.E. teacher.

Quinn, Martha M.
La. L. Rev. 40 859-870 Spr 1980
ARTICLE TYPE: case note
JURISDICTION: Louisiana
Devore v. Hobart Manufacturing Co., 367 So. 2d 836 (La. 1979)
DESCRIPTORS: negligence-cases; tort liability of school districts-
cases

N.Y. Court of Appeals reverses educational malpractice verdict;
misdiagnosis of mental retardation not actionable.
Mental Disab. L. Rep. 4 81 March-April 1980
JURISDICTION: New York
Hoffman v. Board of Education of the City of New York, No. 562
(N.Y. Ct. App. Dec. 17, 1979)
DESCRIPTORS: administrative responsibility-schools; tort liabil-
ity of universities and colleges-constitutional law; United
States. Constitution. 11th Amendment-interpretations and
construction; government liability-constitutional law

Regardless of the search system utilized to gain access to data
(law), the researcher should not disregard the "best of the past,"
when planning the sport law learning experience. Undoubtedly,
it is important and essential to be informed of the changing laws
and their current status. However, valuable lessons may be gained
by comparing cases of similar circumstances separated by several
years, or cases prior to and after significant legislation. As an
example, the courts have approached dress code enforcement, over
the years, in five different patterns (Vacca, R. and Hudgins, H.
C., *Liability of School Officials and Administrators for Civil Rights
Torts, Michie Co., 1982, pp. 235-240)*. Additionally, Title IX legislation (1972), related cases and Grove City provide a solid basis
for discussion about social attitudes, sexual discrimination, Federal funding, etc.

The following resource materials are listed by topics under a
descriptor: i.e., PERIODICALS; Compulsory Attendance; Athletics, Coaches, and the Law; Construction Legislation, Curriculum
Legislation, etc. These resource materials may be of some assistance in drawing from the past for planning a meaningful learning
experience for the future.

PERIODICALS

ACADEMIC FREEDOM

Byse, C. "Academic Freedom, Tenure, and the Law." *American Association Univ. Prof. Bul.* 46:209-17, June, 1960.

Chambers, M.M. "Fantacism Disqualifies A Student Teacher" *College and University*, 35:58-59, Fall, 1959.

Chambers, M.M. "Tumult and the Shouting Diminish," *Educational Forum*, 24:279-83, March, 1960.

Fellman, D. "Academic Freedom in American Public Law." *Teacher College Record*, 62:368-86, February, 1961.

Havighurst, R.J. "I Swear: Levering Act," *School Review*, 59:134-7, March, 1951.

    The loyalty oath may be considered a bar to successful teaching, educational freedom and a handicap to the child.

ATHLETICS, COACHES, AND THE LAW

Carlson, G.T. "I'll Be Suing You Coach," *School Executive*, 76:76-79, April, 1957.

    Presents cases to point up a basic classification of liability principles.

Conway, F.J. "Who's Liable?" *Safety Education*, 2:3-4, Oct., 1960.

    A basic vagueness in liability: profit making school is liable for all acts; charitable organizations seem to be court protected.

Dzenowagis, J.A. "An Accident Reporting System, Why Bother?" *Journal of Health, Physical Education and Recreation*, 33:24, February, 1962

    An accident reporting system may fulfill moral and legal responsibility of safeguarding the student athlete.

Fahr, S.M. "Legal Liability for Athletic Injuries," *Journal of the National Athletic Trainers Association*, Miami Beach, Florida, P. 1-3, June, 1958.

    Tort Liability - Vicarious Liability or Respondent Superior and available defenses.

Garber, Lee O., "Schoolman Can be Sued When Students Ride in His Car," *Nation's Schools*, December 4, 1963.

    The Delaware "Guest Law" - Any nonpaying guest who rides in a car cannot sue for damages, unless the driver causes the accident intentionally.

Garber, L.O. "School District Liability," *American Association of School Administrators Bulletin*, Oct., 1953.

> Governmental Immunity of School Districts as established by common law has been altered by some state legislatures.

Garber, L.O. "The Case of the Negligent Coach," *The Nations' Schools*, 59:77-79, May, 1957.

> Public sentiment may be promoted through newspaper coverage in emergency situations. There is no standard of evaluating behavior in these situations.

Garber, L.O. "Upholds Authority of High School Athletic Association," *Nations Schools*, 65:61, June, 1960.

Garrison, C. "Have You Acted Negligently Today?" *Athletic Journal*, p. 10, December, 1958.

> The teacher must act in a reasonable and prudent manner: Owed a duty, failed to observe the duty, injury occurred, proximate cause must be proven.

Gold, S.Y. "First Aid and Legal Liability," *Journal of Health, Physical Education and Recreation*, 34:42-3, Jan., 1963.

> A prescribed first aid procedure is necessary for the legal protection of the P.E. teacher.

Griffith, John L., "Liability and School Athletics," *Athletic Journal,* pp. 76-98, September, 1964.

> The coach must conform to a standard of behavior reflecting reasonable and prudent action, or negligence may be proven.

Hamilton, R.R. "Contributory Negligence Rule Held Not Applicable to Twelve-Year Old Boy," *The National School Law Reporter*, Vol. 9, No. 15, p. 57.

> A discussion of contributory negligence in a lawsuit with a student injured prior to school hours with power equipment.

Hamilton, R.R. "Dear Subscriber," *The National School Law Reporter,* Vol. IX, No. 14, September 12, 1959.

> This reports an actual case (Welch v. Dunsmuiir) reflecting common place events which precipitated a lawsuit.

Harsha, William N. "Legal Ramification of Athletic Injuries," *The Journal of National Athletic Trainers Association*, 13th Annual Meeting, pp. 15-16, June, 1962.

> Organization of the athletic program should make provision for proper equipment on the release from assumption of risk.

Hunter, O.N. "Liability and the Teacher of Physical Education," Office of Superintendent of Public Instruction, Springfield, Illinois.

    The position of the District has changed through the years: 1959 Molitor vs. Kaneland crumbled the foundations of school district immunity.

Jordan, W.L. "Liability and School Athletics," *Athletic Journal*, pp. 76-92, September, 1963.

    The school must provide the following: organized program, safe environment, proper instruction, and an accident reporting system.

Kigin, Denis J. "Would You Be Liable If . . ." *Safety Education*, Vol. 43, No. 6, pp. 2-7, February, 1964.

    What every teacher should know of liability with emphasis on negligence. (wrestling injury and forseeability)

Lengyel, Jack, "Are You Guilty?" *The Physical Educator*, Vol. 211, No. 3, P. 112, October, 1964.

    It's absolutely necessary to supply the student with safe equipment, safe premises, and eliminate dangerous activities.

Muniz, Arthur J. "The Teacher, Pupil Injury and Legal Liability," *Journal of Health, Physical Education and Recreation*, p. 28, September, 1962.

    Legal protection for the physical educator begins with proper certification, adequate supervision, to teach within rules and regulations.

"Newsletter," *National Organization on Legal Problems in Education*, Topeka, Kansas, Vol. II, III, IV, 1962-64.

    NOLPE presents the recent problems, cases, and decisions in school law.

Nyggard, J.M. "Negligence Can be Costly," *Indiana Teacher*, Vol. 108, No. 7, p. 322, April, 1964.

    There are two basic legal liabilities (1) breach of contract, and (2) tort liability.

Radtke, R.A. "Liability Suit Won by Teacher," *Industrial Arts and Vocational Education*, pp. 130-132, April, 1954.

    Common law principle applied in defense of a student injury liability suit. THe injury occurred in an industrial arts class by an unlabeled and uncorked acid bottle.

Remmlein, M.K. "Legal Authority, Restraints, and Liabilities in Connection with School Camping," *Education*, 73:44-9, Sept., 1952.

    Is camping a part of the school program or is it an ULTRA VIRES activity? Legislation is needed.

Remmlein, M.K. "When Teachers Go To Court," *National Education Association Journal*, 41:105-6, February, 1952.

A presentation of the primary reasons why teachers go to court. (Injuries)

Rice, Sidney "A Suit for the Teacher," *Journal of Health, Physical Education and Recreation*, 32:24-26, November, 1961.

The teacher occupies a position of considerable risk and cannot enjoy the immunity which resides with most school boards.

Roach, Stephen F. "Injuries to Pupils: Is the School Board Liable?" *School Management*, 7:36-40, June, 1963.

The Supreme Court Decisions related to the liability of the school board for injuries to pupils: esp. Respondent Superior.

Rosenfield, Harry N. "Guilty," *Safety Education*, 42:12-16.

It is recommended that governmental immunity be eliminated, school being liable for employee negligence, and insurance should be a part of the school program.

Ryser, Otto E. "Safety, The Administrators and Teacher's Responsibility," *Athletic Journal*, 61:32, Nov., 1960.

"School Laws and Teacher Negligence," *Research Bulletin of the N.E.A.*, 40:75-76, October, 1962.

It is the responsibility of the teacher to plan and program for the safeguard of the student.

Schroyer, George "How's Your Liability Insurance," *School Management*, pp. 91-96, September, 1963.

The value and need of protective insurance as reflected in the transition of district governmental immunity.

Seeley, Darwin. "School Accidents and Teacher Liability," *Journal of School Health*, 32:190-1, May, 1962.

A 1950-60 survey by the Washington State Department of Education showing the incident of accidents and their causes.

"The Codificaiton of School Laws," *Research Bulletin*, National Education Association, Washington, D.C., Vol. 32, Feb., 1954.

A suggested outline for a State School Code: general standards for code statutes, description and evaluation of publications of school law.

Tenue, Moe "The Coaches Legal Liabilities," *Scholastic Coach*, 33:50-56, November, 1963.

Athletic injuries and negligence as related to the coach and his duties.

115

Ware, Martha L. "Is the Teacher Liable?" *National Education Association Journal*, 47:60, December, 1958.
>Cases exemplifying pupil injury and liability.

"Who is Liable for Pupil Injuries?" *National Commission on Safety Education*, Washington, D.C., pp. 1-70, February, 1963.
>The different aspects of liability with illustrative cases to show teacher-student relations in various states.

COMPULSORY ATTENDANCE

Bolmeier, E.C. "Court Decisions and Enrollment Trends in Public and Non-Public Schools," *Elementary School Journal*, 51:70-6, October, 1950.
>Present development portend an acceleration in non-public school growth.

Clark, R.W. "Can Compulsory Attendance Be Enforced?" *Pa. School Journal*, May, 1961.

Davidson, J. "Legal Status of Compulsory School Attendance in Indiana," *Teacher College Journal*, 33:32-3, November, 1961.

_____. "Parent-Teacher Dissociation: Trifan Family," *Time*, 77:41-42, May 5, 1961.

Donahoe, D. "Legislator Looks at Compulsory Attendance Laws," *California Journal of Secondary Education*, 33:106-8, February, 1958.

Garber, L.O. "Court Describes Powers of Attendance Officers," *Nations Schools*, 60:79-80, November, 1957.

_____. "Can Good Teaching Be Illegal? Case of Tommy Kral, Hastings, Minn." *Life*, 46:34, June 29, 1959.

_____. "Cost of Quality: Kral Case." *Time*, 73:68, June 29, 1959.

_____. "School for Tommy Kral," *Time*, 73:31, March 2, 1959.

"State Legislation on School Attendance and Related Matters, School Census and Child Labor," *U.S. Office of Ed.* (OE-24000-Circ. No. 615) 1960.

CONSTRUCTION LEGISLATION; CONTRACTS; ARCHITECTS; etc. See also SCHOOL BOARD LEGISLATION AND ACTION

Garber, L.O. "Board and Architects Disagree about Work in Contract," Nations Schools, 66:70, September, 1960.

Garber, L.O. "Board Scope for Construction Surety Bonds," *Nations Schools*, 63:79, June, 1959.

Garber, L.O. and Tyree, M.J. "Architects Can Recover under Abandoned or Illegal Contracts," *Nations Schools*, 67:122, February, 1961.

Garber, L.O., and Tyree, M.J. "Courts Protect Architect's Investments," *Nations Schools*, 67:81, March , 1961.

Garber, L.O., and Tyree, M.J. "Legal Principles Govern Employment of Architects," *Nations Schools*, 66:90-1, November, 1960.

Garber, L.O., and Tyree, M.J. "Let the Contract Specify Architect's Authority," *Nations Schools*, 66:62-63, December, 1960.

Punke, H.H. "Bid, Performance, and Payment Bonds of School Building Contractors," *American School Board Journal*, 143:40-1, July, 1961.

Punke, H.H. "Payment Bonds," *American School Board Journal*, 143:32-3, August, 1961.

Roach, S.F. "Board Contracts for Architectural Services," *American School Board Journal*, 137:70, February, 1958.

CURRICULUM LEGISLATION & LAWS

Arnold, W.M. "Area Vocational Education Programs," *School Life*, 42:16-21, January, 1960.

Punke, H.H. "Court Rulings on the Curriculum and Teaching Program," *National Association Secondary School Principal's Bulletin*, 43:137-51, December, 1959.

Robinson, G. "Legislation Influence Curriculum Development," Educational Leadership, 19:26-30, October, 1961.

Young, R.J. "Suggested Basis for Examining Legal and Regulatory Requirements Affecting Curriculum," *Educational Administration and Supervision*, 43:395-417, November, 1957.

DISCIPLINE & SCHOOL PERSONNEL

Garber, L.O. "When Is Corporal Punishment Lawful?" *Nations Schools*, 65:100, April, 1960.

Hess, M.M. "Discipline Suit Endangers Career Teacher's Future," *Schools and Community*, 47:17, February.

Masson, J.J. "Can You Punish Your Students?" *Illinois Education*, 47:148, December, 1958.

Punke, H.H. "Corporal Punishment in the Public Schools," *National Association Secondary School Principal's Bulletin,*, 43:118-138, September, 1959.

RESPONSIBILITIES OF DIFFERENT TYPES
OF SCHOOL PERSONNEL

Bolmeier, E.C. "Legal Scope of Teacher's Freedom," *Educational Forum*, 24:199-206, January, 1960.

Bolmeier, E.C. "School Principals' Proper Concept of School Law," Nat. Assn. Sec. Sch. Prin. Bul., 42:1-8, March, 1958.

_____. "Plaintiffs & Defendants: School Teachers in Court," *NEA Research Bulletin*, 36:58-60, April, 1958.

Borchardt, S. "A.F. of T. Aid Program in Washington," *American Teach. Magazine*, 45:7-8, April, 1961.

_____. "Decade of Court Decisions on Teacher Retirement, 1950-1959," *NEA Research Division*, 1960.

Garber, L.O. "Are Union Shop Contracts for Teachers Legal?" *Nations Schools*, 61:70-1, February, 1958.

Garber, L.O. "Labor Board Can Mediate Teacher Salaries," *Nations Schools*, 65:98, Mazarch, 1960.

Garber, L.O. "Needed: Policy for Compounded Maternity Leaves," *Nations Schools*, 66:91, October, 1960.

Garber, L.O. "Supreme Court of Montana Rules Against Teacher's Union," *Nations Schools*, 64:57-8, September, 1959.

_____. "Teacher's Day in Court: Review of 1958-60," *NEA Research Division*, 3v1958, 1959-1960, 1959-61.

Garber, L.O. "Wisconsin Court Defines Legal Responsibilities of School Guidance Counselors," *Nations Schools*, 65:183-6, April, 1960.

Hubbard, Ben C. "School Liability," *Illinois School Board Journal*, November, 1964.

> Liability and school boards, their amount of insurance against loss, Illinois Law, Responsibility of the Boards for employee torts.
>
> Question of Immunity - Modern development of District Liability.

Leipold, L.E. "Law Enters the Classroom," *American School Board Journal*, 118:31-2, April, 1949.

> The right of the teacher to punish a recolcitrant pupil is generally upheld by the courts.

Lightenberg, J. "Teachers' Union and Next Year's Legislations," *American Teach. Magazine,* 43:11-12, December, 1958.

Lightenberg, J. "Courts Hold Tenure Improves School Systems," *American Teach. Magazine*, 43:13-14, December, 1958.

Lightenberg, J. "Teacher Welfare and the Lae," *American Teach. Magazine*, 45:5-6, February, 1961.

_____. "Trends in Teacher Tenure thru Legislation and Court Decision," *NEA Research Division*, 1957.

Roach, S.F. "Board and Workmen's Compensation Benefits," *American School Board Journal*, 134:88, May, 1957.

Roach, S.F. "School District Tort Immunity Overruled," *American School Board Journal*, 139:53, October, 1959.

Soitz, R.C. "Law of Defamation: Tray for the Unwary Schoolman," *American School Board Journal*, 172:13-16, April, 1961.

Stoneking, A. "Teacher Retirement Legislation, 1961," *Illinois Education*, 49:374-5, May, 1961.

Stoneking, W.A. "New Retirement Legislation Benefits Most Teachers," *Illinois Education*, 50:19-30, September, 1961.

FEDERAL LEGISLATION - GENERAL

Dowdey, C."Southerner Looks at the Supreme Court Decision on Segregation," *Saturday Review*, 37:9-10, Oct. 9, 1954.
A look at the South's attitude toward segregation and the intended defiance.

Exton, E. "Federal School Assistance Proposals," *American School Board Journal*, 138:48, April, 1959.

Exton, E. "New Federal Aid Developments," *American School Board Journal*, 140:42-3, April, 1960.

Gauerke, W.E., "Federal Control of State Officials," (In Year Book of School Law) 1958, pp. 139-153.

Hamlin, H.M. "National Policy for Education," *Nations Schools*, 60:38, December, 1957.

Keesecker, W.W. "Supreme Court Decisions Affecting Education," *School Life*, 31:4-7, February, 1949.
Four educational decisions rendered from Founding of court to 1900-about 100 yrs.: Decisions on secret societies, free textbooks in public school, etc.

Keith, E. "Congress Moves Forward," *National Education Association Journal*, 49:16, September, 1960.

_____. "Education Bill Passes Senate: McNamara Bill," *NEA Journal*, 49:3-4, March, 1960.

Knoll, E. "Backstage with the Kennedy Bill," *Overview*, 2:37-8, April, 1961.

Land, W.G. "Federal Education Policy," *Phi Delta Kappen*, 40:106-8, November, 1958.

McCaskill, J.L. "Education & the Congress," *NEA Journal*, 48:66, January, 1959.

McCaskill, J.L. "Obituary on the School Bills," *NEA Journal*, 49:20, October, 1960.

_____. "Two Billion Dollars in a Decade: Public Laws 815 and 847," *School Life*, 43:16-18, April, 1961.

Radcliffe, C.W. "Congressional Activity for Education," *School Life*, 40:7, November, 1957.

_____. "Congressional Proposals for Education," *School Life*, 40:11-14, May, 1958.

Radcliffe, C.W. "Federal Laws for Education: 86th Congress, First Session," *School Life*, 42:22, November, 1959.

Radcliffe, C.W. "Laws for Education: 86th Congress, Second Session," *School Life*, 43:23, November, 1960.

Remmlein, M.K. "Can the Government Legally Control Education?" *School Executive*, 79:64-5, October, 1959.

Rice, A.H. Jr. "Federal Support for Education Stalls on One Yard Line," *Mich. Ed. J.*, 38:12-14, September, 1960.

Robinson, G. "Provisions of Murray-Metcalf Bill," *Nations Schools*, 63:81, March, 1959.

Rodell, F. "School Kids are Colored Blind," *Saturday Review*, 37:9-10, October 16, 1954.

Segregation will ultimately go and is being dismissed with success in many places in the south.

Stiener, A.K. "Educational Legislation," *School Life*, 37:70-1, February, 1955.

This is an emphasis of the significant Legislative Acts: U.S. A.F. Academy - P.L.325; White House Conference - P.L.530.

STATE AND LOCAL LAWS AND LEGISLATION

Eland, I.L. "State Aid for Driver Education," *Safety Education*, 40:15-17, November, 1960.

Eland, I.L. "Assembly Adopts Legislative Program," *Illinois Education*, 49:245-6, February, 1961.

_____. "State School Legislation," (1959) *NEA Research Bulletin*, 37:118-19, December, 1959.

Frederick, W.L. "Education as a Responsibility of the States," *Educational Record*, 39:261-8, July, 1958.

Frederick, W.L. "High Spots in State School Legislation Enacted Jan. 1 - Aug. 1, 1957," *NEA Research Division*, 1957.

Garber, L.O. "Compromise Is Best for City-School District Squabbles," *Nations Schools*, 67:134, May, 1961.

Garber, L.O. "Hands Off on School Matters," *Nations Schools*, 64:84, October, 1959.

New Jersey court tells municipality not to initiate referenda on educational questions.

Garber, L.O. "Illinois Court Overthrows Immunity Doctrine," *Nations Schools*, 64:70-72, August, 1959.

_____. "State School Legislation, 1961," *NEA Research Bulletin*, 39:114-17, December, 1961.

Grimm, L.R. "Legislative Achievements for Education," *Illinois Education*, 48:22-5, September, 1959.

Keesecker, W.W. "State Laws Permitting Wider Use of School Property," *School Life*, 31:3-7, March, 1948.

Pearson, E.F. "Other Legislative Considerations," *Illinois Education*, 49:376, May, 1961.

Roach, S.F. "Compliance with Municipal Codes," *American School Board Journal*, 139:51, September, 1959.

Roach, S.F. "Conflicts between School Districts and Municipalities," *American School Board Journal*, 139:33, July, 1959.

Steiner, A.K. "Report on State Laws, Early Elementary Education," *School Life*, 39:7-10, May, 1957.

_____. "State School Legislation," *NEA Research Bulletin*, 36:113-114, December, 1958.

Steiner, A.K. "State School Legislation 1954," *School Life*, 37:107-8, April, 1955.

    The high points of state legislation for the year 1954; District reorganization, Arizona; educational survey, Nevada, etc.

Talmago, H.E. "Exclusive State Control over Public Education," *School and Society*, 88:243-4, May 7, 1960.

Ware, M.L. "State School Legislation in 1956," *NEA Journal*, 46:546-8, November, 1957.

_____. "State School Legislation, 1957," U.S. Off. of Ed. (Bul 1959 No. 10 Summary in *School Life*, 40:8-9, June, 1958.

FINANCIAL LAWS & LEGISLATION - OTHER THAN NDEA ACTS

Davis, J.V. and Davis, L.R. "Shall We Extend Public Law 874?" *American School Board Journal*, 139:8, July, 1959.

    Federal aid to aimpacted areas.

Huls, H.E. "State Limitations on Local Public School Expenditures in the U.S.," *Journal of Experimental Education*, 27:219-224, March, 1959.

Marston, R.B. "House Will Consider Salary Bill for Teachers," *National Education Association Journal*, 39:259, Apr., 1950.

    The strength and shortcomings in the efforts to pass a Salary Bill for Teachers.

121

McCaskill, J.L. "Children Lose Again," *NEA Journal*, 46:395-7, September, 1957.
Fed. Finance for school construction.
Moyneham, D.P. "Second Look at the School Panic," *Reporter*, 20:14-19, June 11, 1959.
Federal Aid to Education.
Udall, S.L. "Our Education Budget Also Needs Balancing," *Reporter*, 20:23-5, June 25, 1959.
——————. "Principal School Construction Assistance Bills of 1957," *School Life*, 39:10-11, June, 1957.
——————. "School Construction Bill: The Victim is Revived after Being Pronounced Dead Several Times," *Science*, 132:23-4, July 1, 1960.

NDEA ACTS AND LEGISLATION

Lacy, D. "NDEA Act of 1958," *Library Journal*, 84:569-71, February 15, 1959.
Lacy D. "NDEA 1958-1959, A Year of Progress," *School Life*, 42:32-4, October, 1959.
"Loyalty Provisions of NDEA Meet Opposition from Educators and Congressmen," *Science*, 129:625-6, March 6, 1959.
McCarthy, E.J. "Legislation for Education & Defense in the 85th Congress, Second Session," *School Life*, 41:9, Sept., 1958.
——————. "Millions for NDEA and Impacted Areas, Not one Cent for General Support," *NEA Journal*, 50:15-17, October, 1961.
——————. "Proposed Changes in NDEA," *School Life*, 43:3-4, May, 1961.
——————. "Student Loyalty Oath, NDEA," *Commonwealth*, 72:86-8, April 22, 1960.

GENERAL: SEE ALSO FEDERAL AND STATE LEGISLATION

Abels, L.C. "Tort Liability of Iowa School Districts," *Midland Schools*, 74:12-13, April, 1960.
Beach, F.F. and Will, R.F. "State and Nonpublic Schools; with Particular Reference to Responsibility of State Departments of Education," U.S. Office of Ed. (Summary in *School Life*, 40:13-14, February, 1958.
Beutter, E.E. Jr. "Essentials of School Law for Educators," Teacher's College Record, 59:441-9, May, 1958.
Bolmeier, E.C. "Directions in School Law," *American School Board Journal*, 149:33-5, September, 1959.

Brickman, W.W. "Legislative Follies & The Schools," *School and Society*, 86:296, June 21, 1958.

Brown, G.R. "School Legislation: A Perpetual Need," *Illinois Education*, 47:243-5, February, 1959.

Chambers, M.M. "Transfer Credit Cannot Be Withheld," *College and University*, 35 No. 2 pp. 164-65, Winter, 1960.

Chambers, M.M. "Workmen's Compensation for University Employees," *Ed.Research*, 41:183-6, April, 1960.

Edwards, N. "Stability and Change in Basic Concepts of Law Governing American Education," *School Review*, 65:161-175, June, 1957.

Galfo, A. "Keep Your Staff Out of Court," *Overview*, 2:54, April, 1961.

——————. "Standards of School Law," *Times Education Supplement*, 2297:991, May 29, 1959.

Garber, L.O. "Courts Placing More Emphasis on Safe-Harmless Statutes," *Nations Schools*, 59:63-4, June, 1957.

Grimm, L.R. "Digest of New School Laws," *Illinois Education*, 46:21-4, September, 1957.

Kandel, I.L. "Legality of the Feinberg Law," *School and Society*, 70:4-26, December 24, 1949.

The right of the teacher to be in "error of opinion may be tolerated where reason is left to combat it."

Leipold, L.E. "Administrators Agree on 18 Key Problems," *Nations School*, 51:53-4, Feb., 1953.

Outstanding problems mentioned important to sixty administrators: Society, finance, public relations.

Liepold, L.E. "Digest of School Law," *School Executive*, 73:43-7, August, 1954.

An emphasis of the many cases and problems in school administrations which make an understanding of the fundamentals of school law a necessity.

Leipold, L.E. "Four Steps to Understanding School Law," *American School Board Journal*, 136:22-3, June, 1958.

Leipold, L.E. "You Either Have the Right or You Don't," *Clearing House*, 28:69-77, October, 1953.

No arbitrary answer can be given to a question in law for any one particular set of circumstances. General statements of fact are possible.

Loughlin, R.L. "Courage on the Campus," *Nation*, 188:465-6, May 23, 1959.

Tells of rising courage against loyalty oaths, and other types of state and federal controls and regulations.

Loughlin, R.L. "Education is Lawful," *Nat Assn Sec Sch Prin Bulletin*, 44:97-9, March, 1960.
> Gives short rundown on laws and ordinances making education lawful in the U.S.

_____. "Let's Pass a Resolution," *NEA Journal*, 49:20-21, March 7, 1960.
> Tells a way in which a group can express an opinion the strongest way.

Mead, A.R. "Legal Status of Laboratory Schools & Teacher Education Laboratory Practices," *Journal of Teacher Education*, 8:356-64, December, 1957.

Miller, L.N. "Law Case Approach to Ethical Education," *Educational Forum*, 21:421-8, May, 1957.

Pearson, I.F. "IEA Legislative Proposals under Consideration," *Illinois Education*, 47:14-15, September, 1958.

Peterson, C.E. Jr. "After a Decade: Fair Educational Practices Legislation," *College and University*, 36 No. 1, pp. 20-34, Fall, 1960.

Punke, H.H. "Educated Woman & the Legislative Process," *School & Society*, 87:418-20, October 24, 1959.

Radcliffer, C.W. "Adults in the Public Schools," *School Life*, 40:7-10, April, 1958.
> On adult education—includes laws and provisions for adult education in 48 states.

Roach, S.F. "Liberal Court Interpretation of School Statutes," *American School Board Journal*, 138:45, April, 1959.

_____. "School Laws of 1957; Major Enactments in Twenty States," *School Life*, 40:4-7, January, 1958.

_____. "Schools & The Law," *School Executive*, 77:72, Jan. 1958.

Roesch, W.L. "Staffing for School Management: The Legal Aspect," *School Life*, 42:14-15, January, 1960.

_____. "Statutory Basis for Administrative and Specialized Service Staffing in Local School Districts," *U.S. Office of Education* (OE-23,000:Bul 1960 no. 1.)

Sales, M.V. "Some Legal Aspects of Public Summer High Schools," *National Association Secondary School Principles Bulletin*, 45:62-6, February, 1961.

Stonoking, W.A. "Highlights of the 1959 IEA Legislative Program," *Illinois Education*, 47:158-6, December, 1958.

Tressen, D.W. and Foremen, C.M. "Comparative Study of Educational Developments in 1959-60; Free Compulsory Education," *International Yearbook of Education*, 1960, 26-7.

_____. "Student Teaching: Some Legal Considerations," *Teacher Education*, 12:216-218, June, 1961.

Weinstein, G. "Don't Be a Dunce about School Laws," *Better Home and Garden*, 38:166, April, 1960.

HIGHER EDUCATION LEGISLATION

Chambers, M.M. "College Tort Responsibility Since 1950," *Educational Record*, 40:166-172, April, 1959.

Martorana, S.V. "Recent Legislation Proposals Affecting Junior Colleges," *Junior College Journal*, 28:372-9, March, 1958.

Martorana, S.V. "Recent State Legislation Affecting Junior Colleges," *J.C. Journal*, 28:307-21, February, 1958.

_____. "Survey of State Legislation Relating to Higher Education, July 1, 1956-June 30, 1957," J.S. Office of Education, (Circ. No 511), 1957.

Radcliffe, C.W. "Congressional Activity in Higher Education," (First Session, 85th Congress) *Higher Education*, 14:37-9, November, 1957.

_____. "Government Employees Training Act," *Higher Education*, 15:6, September, 1958.

Radcliffe, C.W. "Higher Education in the 86th Congress," *Higher Education*, 16:9-14, November, 1959.

Radcliffe, C.W. "New Legislation of Interest to Higher Education," *Higher Education*, 17:7-8, November, 1960.

_____. "Survey of State Legislation Relating to Higher Education, Jan. 1-Dec. 31, 1960," *U.S. Off. of Ed. Circ.* 647:1-92, 1961.

Skaggs, K.G. "Legislation and Trends in the Centralization of Control of Higher Education at the State Level," *J.C. Journal*, 29:539-44, May, 1959.

"Survey of State Legislation Relating to Higher Education," (July 1, 1957-June 30, 1958 and July 1, 1958-Dec. 31, 1959), *U.S. Off. of Ed. Circ Nos, 552 & 618*.

Thackrey, R.I. and Richter, J. "Land-Grant Colleges and Universities, 1862-1962: An American Institution," *Higher Education*, 16:3-8, November, 1959.

MARRIED STUDENTS

Garber, L.O. "Marriage No Cause for Barring High School Students," *Nations Schools*, 66:66, August, 1960.

Roach, S.F. "Board Rules Concerning Married Students," *American School Board Journal*, 136:56, June, 1958.

PARENTAL AND STUDENT RIGHTS

"Courts Decide Rights and Responsibilities of Pupils," *NEA Research Bulletin*, 36:61-2, April, 1958.

Hubbard, F.W. "Practices, Policies and Parents," *Child Education,*, 34:321-3, March, 1958.

Punke, H.H. "Exclusion of Pupils from Public Schools," *Nat. Assn. Sec. School Prin. Bul*, 42:41-59, September, 1958.

_____. "Pupil's Day in Court, Review of 1957," *NEA Research Division*, 1958.

Rowe, R.N. "Legality of Controls Placed on Clothing Worn by Pupils," *California Journal of Secondary Education*, 35:26-30, January, 1960.

_____. "Pupils Day in Court: Review of 1958-1960," *National Ed. Association Research Bulletin*, 39:41-2, May, 1961.

PAROCHIAL SCHOOLS VS PUBLIC SCHOOLS—ALSO RELIGION & EDUCATION IN GENERAL

Garber, L.O. "Bible Reading Upheld in Miami Public Schools," *Nations Schools*, 67:56-7, June, 1961.

Garber, L.O. "Christmas Creche May Be Placed on School Grounds," *Nations Schools*, 64:82, December, 1959.

Garber, L.O. "Court Defends Under God In Pledge of Allegiance," *Nations Schools*, 60:52-3, August, 1957.

Garber, L.O. "Display of Ten Commandments, Saying Grace Ruled Illegal," *Nations Schools*, 60:45-6, December, 1957.

_____. "School District Gets Stay in Bible Reading Decision," *School Executive*, 79:79, November, 1959.

Gauerke, W.E. "Religion in the Public Schools: Some Legal Problems," *School and Society*, 75:401-4, June 28, 1952.

> The conflicts and implications of the law and the desire to provide study of religion.

"High Court Bars Religious Garb in New Mexico," *National Education Association Journal*, 40:516, November '51.

> Public school teachers may not wear distinctive religious garb in class.

Mulford, H.B., "Illinois Athiest Case," *School and Society*, 65:461-2, June 21, 1947.

> Statute of Illinois impowers school boards - impowered to permit use of public school buildings for public purposes, and has handicapped the state in solving problem of religious instruction.

O'Keefe, W.J., "Status of Parochial & Private Schools under the Law," *National Catholic Education Association Bul.*, 55:291-7, August, 1958.

"Right to Be ignorant," *Scientific American*, 186:38, Feb., 1952. The strength of a pressure group (Christian Science Church) is revealed in a New York Legislature Law.

SCHOOL BOARDS & RELATED AREAS

Garber, L.O. "Boards Bound by Powers Specified in Statutes," *Nations Schools*, 64:62, July, 1959.

Garber, L.O. "Board Has Power to Hire Attorney," *Nations Schools*, 66:70, July, 1960.

Garber, L.O. "Boards Have Much Discretionary Authority," *Nations Schools*, 65:92, May, 1960.

Garber, L.O. "Board Must Adhere to Statute to End Contracts," *Nations Schools*, 61:43, January, 1958.

Garber, L.O. "Citizens Committee Has Advisory Powers Only, Court Rules," *Nations Schools*, 61:77, March, 1958.

Garber, L.O. "How Liable Are School Board Members?" *Nations Schools*, 62:64, December, 1958.

Garber, L.O. "School District Has No Police Powers," *Nations Schools*, 68:48, July, 1961.

Garber, L.O. "Why School Boards Need Legal Counsel," *Nations Schools*, 65:122, February, 1960.

Garber, L.O. "Why Schools Should Find a Competent Attorney, and Follow His Advice," *Nations Schools*, 68: August, 1961.

Hagen, J.W. "Your Special Board Meetings May Be Illegal," *School Executive*, 78:70-71, March, 1959.

Nania, F. "School Boards Can Abolish Secret Societies," *American School Board Journal*, 139:38-9, November, 1959.

Roach, S.F. "Abuse of School Board's Discretionary Authority," *American School Board Journal*, 138:67-8, February, 1959.

Roach, S.F. "Authority to Dismiss a Board Clerk," *American School Board Journal*, 136:56, March, 1958.

Roach, S.F. "Board & Change of Boundry Positions," *American School Board Journal*, 137:21, July, 1958.

Roach, S.F. "Board Employees and Incompatible Officers," *American School Board Journal*, 137:70, February, 1958.

Roach, S.F. "Board & Teacher Transfers," *American School Board Journal*, 135:54, August, 1957.

Roach, S.F. "Election Ballot Propositions for School Construction," *American School Board Journal*, 136:49, January, 1958.

Roach, S.F. "Lawsuits Against School Boards," *American School Board Journal*, 137:58, October, 1958.

Roach, S.F. "Option to Purchase Leases on School Buildings," *American School Board Journal*, 134:63, June, 1957.

Roach, S.F. "Public Places and the Posting of Election Notices," *American School Board Journal*, 135:35, July, 1957.

TRANSPORTATION

Alexander, O., "New Transportation Law," *Illinois Education*, 46:94-5, November, 1957.

Bolmeier, C. "Trends in Pupil Transportation Litigation," *American School Board Journal*, 140:38-40, February, 1960.

Galf, A.J., "Buses and the Law," *Overview*, 1:40-1, August, 1960.

Garber, L.O. "Several Principles of Law Affect Pupil Transportation," *Nations Schools*, 62:41-2, August, 1958.

Punke, H.H., "Recent Court Rulings on Pupil Transportation," *Nat Assn Soc Sch Prin Bulletin*, 45:49-61, February, 1961.

SAFETY

Gauerke, W.E. "School Safety Patrols & the Law," *School Executive*, 77:67-71, December, 1957.

——————. "Study Examines Laws on Safety Education," *Safety Education*, 41:24, September, 1961.

SPECIAL EDUCATION

Alpren, M. and Hohenstein, C., "Survey of Provisions for the Gifted at the State Level," *Exceptional Child*, 26:292-4, May, 1960.

Conner, L.E. "CIC's Federal Legislative Activity," *Exceptional Child*, 28:135-9, November, 1961.

Garber, L.O. "Responsibility for Educable," *Nations Schools*, 64:84, November, 1959.

Goldbert, I.I., "Some Aspects of the Current Status of Education and Training in the U.S. for Trainable Mentally Retarded Children," 24:246-54, December, 1957.

Simches, R.F. and Cicenia, E.F., "Home Teaching Provisions at the State Level," *Exceptional Child*, 25:11-15, September, 1958.

Books

Abbott, Edith, *Truancy and Non-Attendance in the Chicago Schools*, Chicago, The University of Chicago Press, 1917.

Allen, Hollis, *The Federal Government and Education*, New York, McGraw Hill Book Co., Inc., 1950.

American Association of School Administrators, *School District Liability*, Washington, D.C., 1953.

Barrett, Vince F., "Liability in Athletics in Oregon," *Research Quarterly*, March, 1939, pp. 99-101.

Beecher, Dwight E., *The New York State Teachers' Salary Law of 1947*, 1949.

Benedetti, Eugene, *School Law Materials*, Dubuque, Iowa, Wm. C. Brown Co., 1961.

Black, Henry Campbell, *Black's Law Dictionary*, 3rd Edition, St. Paul, Minnesota, West Publishing Co., 1933.

Boles, Donald E., *The Bible, Religion and the Public Schools*, Ames, Iowa, Iowa State University Press, 1961.

Bolin, John G., *Review of court Cases Concerning Illinois Public Schools, Personnel and Law 1945-1960*, Normal, Illinois State Normal University, 1961.

Burt, Lorin A., *School Law and the Indiana Teacher*, Bloomington, Indiana, Beanblossom Publishers, 1962.

California Teachers Association, *Teachers Legal Guide*, California Teachers Association Press, 1957.

Chambers, M.M., *The Colleges and the Courts Since 1950*, Danville, Illinois Interstate Press, 1964.

Codification of the School Laws of Illinois, Chicago, Illinois, 1945.

Compulsory School Attendance and Minimum Education Requirements in the United States, Washington, D.C., 1950.

Drury, Robert L., *Drurys' Ohio School Guide - Second Edition*, Cincinnati, Ohio, W.H. Anderson Co., 1960.

Duke University School of Law, *Law and Contemporary Problems*, Vol. 20, No. 1, Durham, North Carolina, 1955.

Dyer, D.E., and Lichtig, L.G., *Liability in Public Recreation*, Appleton, Wisconsin, Nelson Publishing Co., 1949.

Educational Legislation, 1910-date, U.S. Bureau of Education, Washington, D.C.

Edwards, Newton, *The Courts and the Public Schools*, (The Legal Basis of School Organization and Administration) Chicago, University of Chicago Press, 1955.

Fellman, David, *The Supreme Court and Education*, New York Teachers College, Columbia University, 1960.

Garber, Drury and Shaw, *The Law and the Ohio Teacher*, Danville, Illinois, Interstate Publisher and Printers, 1956.

Garber, Lee O., *Handbook of School Law*, Conneticut, Arthur C. Croft, 1954.

Garber, Lee O., *Law and the School Business Manager*, Danville, Illinois, Interstate Printers and Publishers, 1957.

Garber, Lee O., "Origin of the Governmental Immunity from Tort Doctrine," *1964 Yearbook of School Law*, Danville, Illinois, Interstate Printers and Publishers, Inc., 1962.

Garber, Lee O., *The Yearbook of School Law, 1962*, (1st Edition, 1933) Danville, Illinois, Interstate Printers and Publishers, Inc., 1962.

Garber, Lee O., and Edwards, N., *Law Governing Teaching Personnel*, School Law Casebook 3#, Danville, Illinois, Interstate Printers and Publishers, 1962.

Gauerke, Warren, *Legal and Ethical Responsibility of School Personnel*, New Jersey, Prentice Hall, Inc., 1959.

Hales, Dawson, *Federal Government Control of Public Education*, New York, Bureau of Publications, Teachers College, 1954.

Hamilton, R.R., *Bi-Weekly School Law Letter*, Larainie, University of Wyoming, 1951-55.

Hamilton, R.R., *Selected Legal Problems in Providing Federal Aid for Education*, Washington, D.C., U.S. Government Printing Office, 1938.

Hamilton, R.R. and Reutter, Edmund, *Legal Aspects of School Board Operation*, Teachers College, 1958.

Harper, Fowler V., *A Treatise on the Law of Torts*, Bobbs-Merrill Co., 1933.

Harper, Fowler V. and Fleming, James, *The Law of Torts*, Boston, Mass., Little, Brown and Co., 1956.

Henry, Nelson B., and Korwin, J.G., *Schools and City Government*, 1938.

Huston, Wendell, *School Laws of the Forty-Eight States*, Seattle, Washington, Huston Co., 1941.

Illinois School Law as Found in the Statutory Provisions, the Decisions of the Supreme Court and Appellate Courts, etc., Samuel S. DuHamel (Ed.), Springfield, Illinois, 1926.

Johnson, Alvin and Yest, Frank, *Separation of Church and State*, University of Minnesota Press, 1948.

Keesecker, W.W., *Compulsory School Attendance and Minimum Educational Requirements in the U.S.*, Circular #40, Washington, D.C., 1950.

Lemmer, K.H., Friedman, S.L., *The School Code of Illinois*, Springfield, Illinois, Department of Public Instruction, 1959.

Libner, Dorothy and Raymond, *General and Legal Aspects of a School Building Program*, 1951.

Lloyd, F.S., Deaver, G.G. and Eastwood, L.D., *Safety in Athletics*, Chap. VII, W.B. Saunders Co., 1939.

Lloyd, F.S., *Safety in Physical Education in Secondary Education*, New York, National Bureau of Casualty and Surety Underwriters, 1933.

Marke, David Taylor, *Educational Law Simplified*, New York, Oceana Publications, 1949.

Matzer, John M., *State Constitutional Provisions for Education*, (Fundamental Attitudes of American people, 1776-1929) 1931.

Messich, John D., *The Discretionary Powers of School Boards*, 1949.

National Education Association, *Teachers Liability for Pupil Injury*, Washington D.C., 1941, p. 24.

National Safety Council, *Safety in Physical Education and Recreation*, 1941.

Perry, Arthur C., *The Status of the Teacher*, New York, Houghton Mifflin Co., 1912.

Proctor, Arthur, *Safeguarding the School Board's Purchase of Architects Working Drawings*, New York, Teachers College, Columbia University, 1931.

Punke, Harold H., *Community Uses of Public School Facilities*, New York, King's Crown Press, 1951.

Punke, Harold H., *The Courts and School Property*, Chicago, University of Chicago Press, 1936.

Punke, Harold H., *Law and Liability in Pupil Transportation*, Chicago, Illinois, University of Chicago Press, 1943.

Remmlein, M.K., *The Law of Local Public School Administration*, New York, McGraw Hill Book Co., Inc., 1953.

Remmlein, M.K. and Rezny, A.A., *A Schoolman in the Law Library*, Danville, Illinois, Interstate Printers and Publishers, 1962.

Remmlein, M.K. and Ware, M.L., *An Evaluation of Existing Forms of School Laws*, Cincinnati, Ohio, W.H. Anderson Co., 1959.

Reutter, E. Edmund, Jr., *The School Administrator and Subversive Activities*, 1951.

Reutter, E. Edmund, Jr., *Schools and the Law*, New York, Oceana Publications, Inc., 1960.

Reynolds, T.A., *School Laws and Legislation - Illinois*, Springfield, Illinois, State of Illinois, 1959.

Schaerer, R.W. and McGheney, M.A., *Tort Liability of School Districts*, Bloomington, Indiana, Beanblossom Publishers, 1960.

Seaton, D.C., *Safety in Sports*, New York, Prentice Hall, Inc., 1949.

Seaton, D.C., *Safety in Sports,* New York, Prentice Hall, Inc., 1949.

Seitz, Reynolds C., *Law and the Principal,* Cincinnati, Ohio, W.H. Anderson Co.

Smith, J.H., *Legal Limitations on Bonds and Taxation for Public School Buildings,* New York, Columbia University, 1930.

Soper, Wayne W., *Legal Limitations on the Rights and Powers of School Boards with Respect to Taxation,* 1929.

Spurlock, Clark, *Education and the Supreme Court,* Urbana, University of Illinois Press, 1955.

Terry, Paul W., *Legislation on the Junior High School,* Washington, D.C., Government Printing Office, 1924.

Truslor, Harry R., *Essentials of School Law,* Milwaukee, Wisconsin, Bruce Publishing Co., 1927.

Umbeck, Nelda R., *State Legislation on School Attendance and Related Matter, School Census and Child Labor,* Washington, D.C., U.S. Office of Education, 1960.

United States Dept. of Health, Education and Welfare, *Know Your School Law,* Washington, D.C., U.S. Printing Office, No. 8, Bulletin, 1958.

_____, *The State and Education,* Washington D.C., U.S. Printing Office, 1955.

_____, *State Legislation on School Attendance,* Washington D.C., U.S. Printing Office, Circular No. 65, Jan. 1-60, 1960.

_____, *The State and Nonpublic Schools,* Washington D.C., U.S. Printing Office, 1955.

Voorhees, Harvey C., *The Law of the Public School System of the United States,* Boston, Mass., Little, Brown and Co., 1916.

Wells, M.M. and Taylor, P.S., *The New Law of Education,* London, Butterworth and Co., 1954.

Weltzin, Frederick, *The Legal Authority of the American Public School,* 1930.

White, Frank S., *Constitutional Provision for Differential Education,* Fairmont, West Virginia, 1950.

Williams, J.F. and Brownwell, C.L., *The Administration of Health and Physical Education,* W.B. Saunders Co., Chap. IV, pp. 60-65, 1946.

BOOKS — ANNOTATED

Baker, Robert E., *The Implications of School Liability for Teachers of Health Education in New York City,* New York, Columbia University, pp. 163, 1956.

> Aims to give an understanding of liability and its affect on schools by discussing accidents, their elimination and legal involvements.

Corbin, Dan H., *REcreation Leadership,* New York, Prewntice Hall, Inc., 1953.

Recreation leaders are liable whether he is present or not, in administering first-aid and crowded playgrounds.

Edwards, Newton, *The Courts and the Public Schools,* Chicago, IL, University Press, 1933.

Educational systems have become major public enterprises and law and legal decisions have a direct effect on the operation of the school units.

Flowers, Anne and Bolmeier, Edward, *Law and Public Control,* Cincinnati, Ohio, W.H. Anderson Co., pp. 71-89, 1964.

Cases and rulings as they affect dress and appearance in Physical Education Classes.

Fulbright, Evelyn R. and Bolmeier, Edward C., *Courts and The Curriculum,* Cincinnati, Ohio, W.H. Anderson, pp. 54-61, 1964.

Discussion and rulings on athletic facilities and the authority to ban athletics from school.

Guley, Marc, *The Legal Aspects of Injuries in Physical Education and Athletics,* Syracuse University, pp. 39-41, 1952.

To establish liability must prove (1) whether or not there has been negligence, (2) whether there are supervening rules of law which exempt even the one guilty of negligence from financial liability, (3) plaintiff in no way contributed to injury, (4) teacher negligence was the proximate cause.

Hamilton, R.R., *Legal Rights and Liabilities of Teachers,* Laramie, Wyoming, School Law Publications, p. 95, 1956.

Legal nature of the school: teacher and district liable for breach of contract; teacher individually liable for his torts; *reasonable* corporal punishment may be inflicted; legal danger in using personal auto for school business.

Hamilton, R.R. and Mort, Paul R., *The Law and Public Education,* Foundation Press Inc., pp. 273-275.

Everyone, regardless of position, is liable for his own actions. This is especially true of teachers exposed to high numbers of activities engaged in by students.

Jayner, S.C., "Tort Liability and the Common Law Principle of Governmental Immunity," *Report on Insuring,* Kalamazoo, Michigan, Association of School Business, pp. 5-12, 1948.

Through the years districts were immune to actions in tort unless specified by statutes and laws to the contrary.

Kunstler, William M., *The Law of Accidents*, New York, Oceana
Publications, Chap. III, pp. 20-25.
> The proximate cause limiting a persons liability for the
> consequences of his conduct.

Nolte, M. Chester and Linn, John P., *School Law for Teachers*,
Danville, Illinois, Interstate Printers and Publishers Inc., pp.
241-269, 1963.
> Legal test for a tortious act: (1) existence of legal duty to
> another, (2) breach of duty, (3) casual link between the
> breach and the distress of the injured.

Poe, Arthur Clayton, *School Liability for Injuries to Pupils, A
Study of the Legal Liability for the Injury of Children in Public
Schools*, New York, Columbia University, p. 108, 1941.
> A presentation of studies, interpretations of legal princi-
> ples, damages, who's liable, negligence, and contributory
> negligence.

Prosser, William L., *Law of Torts*, Mann Publishing Co., p. 185,
1963.
> A report of various cases; some discussion on the duty to
> come to the assistance of a person in peril (none); a duty
> to avoid any act which makes the situation worse (yes).

Punke, Harold H., "Federal Aid for Educational Projects," *The
Seventh Yearbook of School Year*, Chap. 10, p. 94, 1939.
> A loaned servant does not become the servant of the bor-
> rower unless the borrower has exclusive control over the
> instructor.

Remmlein, M.K., *School Law*, New York, McGraw Hill Book Co.,
pp. 152-154, 1950.
> Teachers are liable for pupil injury, but the extent to
> which they are liable for injuries depends upon common
> law principles of negligence. (case reports)

Rosenfield, Harry N., *Liability for School Accidents*, New York,
Harper Bros., 1940.
> The discussion centers around negligence and types of
> insurance (bodily injury and property damage) with em-
> phasis provided by case reports.

Voltmer, E.F., and Esslinger, A.A., *The Organization and Administration of Physical Education*, New York, F.S. Crafts and
Co., 1938.
> Section related to legal liability for injury.

GLOSSARY

LEGAL TERMS PERTAINING TO SCHOOL LAW[1]

AB INITO. From the beginning.

ACTION. An ordinary proceeding in a court by which one party prosecutes another for the enforcement or protection of a right, the redress of a wrong, or the punishment of a public offense. In common language, a "suit" or "lawsuit."

ACTION AT LAW. Court action in a law case, as distinguished from equity.

AD LITEM. For the purpose of the suit; a guardian AD LITEM is a guardian appointed to prosecute or defend a suit on behalf of someone incapacitated by infancy or otherwise.

ALIUNDE. From another source; from outside.

ALLEGATION. Statement in pleadings setting forth what the party expects to prove.

ALLEGE. To state, assert, or charge; to make an allegation.

AMICUS CURIE. Friend of the court; a counselor who interposes and volunteers information upon some matter of law in regard to which the court is doubtful or mistaken.

Black, Henry Campbell, BLACK'S LAW DICTIONARY, West Publishing Co., St. Paul, Minnesota, 1933.

ANNOTATION. Notes or commentaries in addition to the principal text. A book is said to be annotated when it contains such notes.

APPELLANT. The party who takes an appeal from one court to another.

APPELLEE. The party against whom an appeal is taken.

ARBITRARY. Not supported by fair cause and without reason given.

ASSAULT. An attempt to beat another, without touching him. See BATTERY.

---

[1]Remmlein, Madaline K., SCHOOL LAW, Appendix C. McGraw-Hill Book Co., New York, 1950, pp. 359-366.

AVOID A CONTRACT. To cancel and make the contract void.

BATTERY. An unlawful beating or other wrongful physical violence inflicted on another without his consent. The offer or attempt to commit a battery is an assault. There can be an assault without a battery; battery always includes assault. The two words are usually used together.

BILL. A written complaint filed in a court.

BONA FIED. In or with good faith; honestly, openly, and sincerely; without deceit or fraud.

BREACH OF CONTRACT. Failure without legal excuse to perform part of the whole contract.

CAVEAT EMPTOR. Let the buyer beware.

CERTIFICATE. A document designed as notice that some act has been done, or some event occurred, or some legal formality complied with; evidence of qualification.

CERTIORARI (WRIT OF). The name of a writ issued by a superior court directing an inferior court to send up records and proceedings in a case before verdict, with its certificate to the correctness and completeness of the record for review or retrial.

CITATIONS. References to law books. A citation includes the book where the reference is found, the volume number, and section or page numbers. A uniform system of abbreviations in case law has been adopted, but statutory materials differ from state to state according to the official designation accepted by the legislature.

CITATIONS, JUDICIAL. References to court decisions. Citations in the case material in this text refer to official state reports and to the National Reporter System. The volume number precede the abbreviation of the reporter, and the page number follows it. In parentheses is the name of the state where the decision was rendered and its date. A complete judicial citation includes everywhere that the case may be found, but for school-law work complete parallel citations are unnecessary.

CITATIONS, STATUTORY. References to statutes; where the statute may be found in publicly available form. Statutory citations in this text include the name of the column, the title and/or chapter, and section numbers quoted.

CIVIL ACTION. One brought to recover some civil right, or to obtain redress for some wrong.

CLASS BILL OR SUIT. A case in which one or more in a numerous class, having a common interest in the issue, sue in behalf of themselves and all others of the class.

CODE. A compliance of statutes, scientifically arranged into chapters, subheadings, and section, with a table of contents and index.

CODIFICATION. Process of collecting and arranging the laws of a state into a code.

COLLATERAL ATTACK. An attempt to destroy the effect of a judgment by reopening the merits of a case or by showing reasons why the judgement should not have been given, in an action other than that in which the judgment was given; that is, not in an appeal.

COMMON LAW. As used in this text, legal principles derived from usage and customs, or from court decisions affirming such usages and customs, or the acts of Parliament in force at the time of the American Revolution, as distinguished from law created by enactment of American legislatures.

CONCURRENT JURISDICTION. Two courts having the same authority.

CONCURRING OPINION. An opinion written by a judge who agrees with the majority of the court as to the decision in a case, but has different reasons for arriving at that decision.

CONSIDERATION IN CONTRACTS. The inducement, usually an amount of money.

CONSTITUTION. The supreme organic and fundamental law of a nation or state, establishing the character and conception of its government, laying the basic principles to which its internal life is to be conformed, organizing the government, and regulating, distributing, and limiting the functions of its different departments, and prescribing the extent and manner of the exercise of sovereign powers.

CONTRACT. An agreement upon sufficient consideration, to do or not to do a particular thing; the writing which contains the agreement of the parties, with the terms and conditions, and which serves as proof of the obligation.

CONTRACT ACTION. An action brought to enforce rights under a contract.

CREDIBILITY OF WITNESSES. Worthiness of belief of testimony of witnesses.

CRIMINAL ACTION. Proceeding by which a party charged with a crime is brought to trial and punishment.

DAMAGES. Pecuniary compensation or indemnity which may be recovered in court by the person who has suffered loss or injury to his person, property, or rights through the unlawful act, omission, or negligence of another.

DE FACTO. In fact; actually.

DE FACTO OFFICER. One who is in actual possession of an office without lawful title; as opposed to a DE JURE OFFICER.

DE JURE. Legitimate; lawful.

DE JURE OFFICER. One who has just claim and rightful title to an office, although not necessarily in actual possession thereof.

DECLARATORY RELIEF. A judgment which declares the rights of the parties or expresses the opinion of the court on a question of law, without ordering anything to be done.

DECREE. Order of the court of equity announcing the legal consequences of the facts found.

DEFENDANT. The party against whom relief or recovery is sought in a court action.

DEFENDANT IN ERROR. Defendant in appellate court when the "appeal" is for review on writ or error.

DEFENSE. That which is offered and alleged by the defendant as a reason in law or fact why the plaintiff should not recover.

DEMURRER. To admit the facts as stated, but insisting that there is no cause for action. Note: It is always the defendant who does the demurring. The lower court might sustain the demurrer, and the case will be appealed.

DESCRIPTIO PERSONAE. A word or phrase used merely for the purpose of identifying or pointing out the person intended.

DIRECTORY. An instruction of no obligatory force and involving no invalidating consequences for its disregard.

DISMISSED FOR WANT OF EQUITY. Case dismissed because the allegations in the complaint have been found untrue, or because they are insufficient to entitle complainant to the relief sought.

DISSENTINO OPINION. The opinion in which a judge announces his dissent from the conclusions held by the majority of the court.

DIVISIBLE CONTRACT. One which can be separated into two or more parts not necessarily dependent on each other not intended by the parties to be so.

DISCRIMINATION, UNCONSTITUTIONAL. The effect of a statute which confers particular privileges on a class arbitrarily selected and for whom no reasonable distinction can be found.

DUE PROCESS. The exercise of the powers of government in such a way as to protect individual rights.

EJUSDEM GENERIS. Of the same kind, class, or nature. In statutory construction the EJUSDEM GENERIS rule is that, where general words follow an enumeration of words of a particular and specific meaning, the general words are not interpreted in their widest sense but as applying to persons or things of the same general kind or class as those specifically mentioned.

EMANCIPATION OF CHILD. Surrender of the right to care, custody, and earnings of a child by its parents who at the same time renounce parental duties.

ENFORCEABLE CONTRACT. Any contract not void or voidable because defective.

ENJOIN. To require a person, by writ of injunction from a court of equity, to perform, or to abstain or desist from, some act.

EQUITABLE RELIEF. Decree in court of equity.

EQUITY. As used in this text, the field of jurisprudence differing, in origin, theory, and methods from the common law.

ESTOP. To prevent.

ESTOPPEL. A bar raised by the law which prevents a man from alleging or denying a certain fact because of his previous statement or conduct.

EX DELICTO. From a tort, fault, or malfeasance.

EX PARTE. On one side only; a judicial proceeding, order, injunction when granted for the benefit of one party only.

EX POST FACTO. After the fact. An ex post facto law is one passed after an act which retrospectively changes the legal consequences of that act. The Federal constitution prohibits the passage of ex post facto laws, referring to criminal laws only.

EX REL. Abbreviation for EX RELATIONE, meaning on relation or information. For the purpose of this test, it needs to be explained only as designating a type of court action.

EX VI TERMINI. From the very meaning of the expression used; ascertainable in one way only.

EXCEPTION. In civil procedure, a formal objection to the action of the court when it refuses a request or overrules an objection, implying that the party excepting does not acquiesce in the court's ruling and may base an appeal thereon.

EXECUTED CONTRACT. An incompletely performed contract; something yet to be done in the future.

HEARING ON THE MERITS. Trial on the substance of a case as opposed to consideration of procedure only.

HEARSAY EVIDENCE. Testimony given by a witness who related what others have told him or what he has heard said by others, rather than what he knows personally.

IN LOCO PARENTIS. In place of the parent; charged with some of the parent's rights, duties, and responsibilities.

IN PARI DELICTO. In equal fault; equally culpable or criminal.

IN PERSONAM. Action against the person.

IN RE. Concerning. When used in a title of a court case, it merely designates a type of case.

IN REM. Action instituted against a thing; proceedings taken directly against property.

IN STATU QUO. In the condition in which it was.

INDIVISIBLE CONTRACT. One which forms a whole, the performance of every part of condition precedent to bind the other party; as opposed to a divisible contract which is composed of independent parts the performance of any one of which will bind the other party as far as it goes.

INFORMATION. An accusation against a person.

INJUNCTION. A prohibitive writ issued by a court of equity forbidding the defendant to do some act he is threatening, or forbidding him to continue doing some act which is injurious to the plaintiff and cannot be adequately redressed by an action at law.

INJUNCTION, TEMPORARY. An injunction granted at the beginning of a suit to restrain the defendant from doing some act, the right to which is in dispute, and which may be discharged or made permanent according to the result of the case after the rights of the parties are determined.

INTER ALIA. Among other things.

INVALID. Not binding; lacking in authority.

IPSO FACTO. By the fact itself; by the mere fact.

LACHES. Omission to assert a right for an unreasonable and unexplained length of time, under circumstances prejudicial to the adverse party.

LAW. (1) System of principles or rules of human conduct. In this sense it includes decisions of courts as well as acts of legislatures. (2) An enactment of a legislature, a statute.

LEGAL DISABILITY. Lack of legal capacity to perform an act.

LEGAL POWER. The right or ability to do some act.

LIABILITY. Legal responsibility.

LIQUIDATED DAMAGES. A specific sum of money stipulated by the parties by bond or contract as the amount of damages to be recovered by one party for breach of the agreement by the other.

MAJORITY OPINION. The statement of reasons for the views of the majority of the members of the bench in a decision in which some of them disagree.

MAJORITY RULE. A legal principle upheld by the majority of decisions on the question, when there are a lesser number of decisions to the contrary on the same issue.

MALFEASANCE. Commission of an unlawful act.

MALUM IN SE. A wrong in itself.

MALUM PROHIBITUM. An act which is wrong because prohibited.

MANDAMUS. A compulsory, referring a command for which disregard or disobedience is lawful.

MANDATORY. Compulsory, referring to a command for which disregard or disobedience is lawful.

MINORITY RULE. The principle upheld by some courts on an issue which has been decided to the contrary by the majority of courts.

MISFEASANCE. Improper performance of some lawful act; negligence.

NON OBSTAUTE VEREDICTO. Notwithstanding the verdict.

NON SEQUITOR. It does not follow; a fallacious conclusion.

NONFEASANCE. Failure a person to do some act which he ought to do.

NOLENS VOLENS. With or without consent.

NONSUIT. Judgment against a plaintiff when he is unable to prove a case, or when he neglects to proceed to the trial of a case after it has been put in issue.

OBITER DICTUM. An opinion of the court not necessary to the judgment given of record, and consequently of less authority.

PARI MATERIA. Of the same matter; on the same subject.

PAROL-EVIDENCE RULE. Oral evidence as to matters not contained in a written contract or other instrument is not admissable.

PEREMPTORY. Absolute; final; positive; not requiring any cause to be withdrawn.

PER SE. In itself; inherently; unconnected with other matters.

PERSUASIVE VALUE. Influence of decisions of one jurisdiction in another jurisdiction.

PETITION. Written application or prayer to the court for the redress of a wrong or the grant of a privilege or license.

PETITIONER. The one who presents a petition to the court; same as plaintiff in other kinds of cases.

PLAINTIFF. Person who brings an action; he who sues by filing a complaint.

PLAINTIFF IN ERROR. The party who sues out a writ of error to review a judgment or other proceeding at law.

PLEA. A suit or action.

PLEA IBATEMENT. An objection to the place, method, or time of plaintiff's assertion of a claim, without disputing the justice of the claim.

PLEAD. To make, deliver, or file any pleading.

PLEADINGS. Formal papers filed in court action including complaint by plaintiff and defendant's answer showing what is alleged on one side and admitted or denied on the other side.

PLENARY. Entire; complete; unabridged.

POLICE POWER. As used in this text, legislative power to enact laws for the comfort, health, and prosperity of the state.

PRAYER. The part of the petition in which petitioner requests the court to grant the relief sought.

PRECEDENT. A decision considered as furnishing an example or authority for an identical or similar case afterward arising on a similar question of law.

PRIMA FACIE CASE. A case in which the evidence is so strong that the adverse party can overthrow the evidence only by sufficient rebutting evidence.

PRIVIES OF PARTIES. Persons connected with mutual interest in the same action.

PRO TANTO. For so much; for so much as may be.

QUANTUM MERUIT. An implication that the defendant had promised to pay plaintiff as much as he reasonably deserved for work or labor.

QUANTUM VALEBANT. As much as they are worth.

QUASI. As if; as it were; analogous to.

QUA WARRANTO. Information in the nature of a QUO WARRANTO. Method of trying title to a public office.

QUO ANIMO. With what intention or motive.

QUO WARRANTO. By what authority.

RATIFICATION. Confirmation of a transaction by one who before ratification had the optional right to relieve himself of its obligation.

REGULATIONS. Rules for management or government.

RELATOR. Person upon whose complaint writs are issued, and who is quasi the plaintiff.

RELIEF. The redress or assistance which a complainant seeks from the court; not properly applied to money damages.

REMAND A CASE. To send the case back to the court from which it came for further proceedings there, after an appellate decision.

RES ADJUDICATA. A matter judically decided.

RES IPSA LOQUITUR. The thing speaks for itself; rebuttable presumption that defendant was negligent.

RES JUDICATA. A matter adjudged; a thing judicially acted upon or decided.

RES NOVA. A new matter; a question not before decided.

RECISSION OF CONTRACT. Cancellation or abrogation by the parties, or one of them.

RESPONDENT. Defendant in certain kinds of cases.

RESPONDENT SUPERIOR. The master is liable in certain cases for the wrongful acts of his servant; let the master answer.

RESTRAIN. To prohibit from action; to enjoin.

RIGHT. A power or privilege in one person against another.

STARE DECISIS. Principle that when a court has made a declaration of a legal principle, it is the law until changed by competent authority; upholding of precedents within the jurisdiction.

STATUTE. Act of the legislation.

STIPULATION. (1) A particular provision in an agreement; (2) An agreement between counsel concerning business before a court.

STRICTISSIMI JURIS. Of the strictest right or law.

SUFFICIENCY OF EVIDENCE. Evidence adequate in character, weight, or amount to justify legal action sought.

SUPERSEDEAS. A writ by an appellate court containing a command to stay the proceedings at law.

TENURE. In its general sense, made of holding an office or position, especially with respect to time.

TORT. Legal wrong committed upon the person or property of another independent of contract.

ULTRA VIRES. Acts beyond the scope of authority.

VALIDITY. Legal sufficiency in contradistinction to more regularity.

VENUE. Place in which an injury is declared to have been done, or fact declared to have happened.

VESTER RIGHT. A right which has so completely and definitely accrued or settled in a person that it cannot be cancelled or impaired.

VOID. Ineffectual, having no legal force or binding effect; said of a contract so defective that nothing can cure it.

VOIDABLE. That which may be avoided or declared void; as to contracts, a defective instrument which can be cured by ratification by the one who could have avoided it.

WRIT OF MANDAMUS. Command; a writ issued by a court of superior jurisdiction, commanding the performance of a certain act.

WRIT IN VACATION. Court order issued during intermission of court session.